Rethinking Global Value Chains and Corporate Social Responsibility

RETHINKING BUSINESS AND MANAGEMENT

The Rethinking Business and Management series is a forum for innovative scholarly writing from across all substantive fields within business and management. The series aims to enrich scholarly inquiry by promoting a cutting-edge approach to management theory and analysis.

Despite the old maxim that nothing is new under the sun, it is nevertheless true that organisations evolve and contexts in which businesses operate change. Business and Management faces new and previously unforeseen challenges, responds to shifting motivations and is shaped by competing interests and experiences. Academic scrutiny and challenge is an essential component in the development of business theory and practice and the act of re-thinking and re-examining principles and precepts that may have been long-held is imperative.

Rethinking Business and Management showcases authored books that address their field from a new angle, expose the weaknesses of existing frameworks, or "re-frame" the topic in some way. This might be through the integration of perspectives from other fields or even other disciplines, through challenging existing paradigms, or simply through a level of analysis that elevates or sharpens our understanding of a subject. While each book takes its own approach, all the titles in the series use an analytical lens to open up new thinking.

Rethinking Global Value Chains and Corporate Social Responsibility

Peter Lund-Thomsen

Professor of Corporate Social Responsibility in Developing Countries, Center for Business and Development Studies, Department of Management, Communication and Society, Copenhagen Business School, Denmark

RETHINKING BUSINESS AND MANAGEMENT

 Edward Elgar
PUBLISHING

Cheltenham, UK • Northampton, MA, USA

Cover image: Remy Gieling on Unsplash

Published by
Edward Elgar Publishing Limited
The Lypiatts
15 Lansdown Road
Cheltenham
Glos GL50 2JA
UK

Edward Elgar Publishing, Inc.
William Pratt House
9 Dewey Court
Northampton
Massachusetts 01060
USA

Paperback edition 2023

A catalogue record for this book
is available from the British Library

Library of Congress Control Number: 2022931708

This book is available electronically in the **Elgar**online
Business subject collection
http://dx.doi.org/10.4337/9781839102097

ISBN 978 1 83910 208 0 (cased)
ISBN 978 1 83910 209 7 (eBook)
ISBN 978 1 0353 2740 9 (paperback)
Printed and bound by CPI Group (UK) Ltd, Croydon, CR0 4YY

Contents

Preface and acknowledgements   vi

1   Introduction: rethinking global value chains and corporate social responsibility   1

2   Buyer perspectives   23

3   Supplier-centered perspectives   40

4   Cluster-centered perspectives   49

5   Worker-centered perspectives   64

6   Conclusion: corporate social responsibility in global value chains towards 2030   88

References   106

Index   120

Preface and acknowledgements

This book has mainly been written during a second lock-down in Copenhagen, Denmark in January and February 2021. Originally, I had planned on writing a book with the title "Rethinking global value chains and sustainability (GVCs)" after I had been approached by Edward Elgar Publishing in 2019 with the idea of authoring a book for their "Rethinking series." However, after I had obtained a grant from their Carlsberg Foundation later in 2019 to write the book, COVID-19 erupted in early 2020 and had substantial impacts on how I conceptualized the book.

First, it appeared to me that COVID-19 seemed to reinforce some of the earlier trends underlying GVC analysis that we were already familiar with. The power of multinational companies to influence the operations of their vast networks of suppliers became particularly obvious, as many lead firms temporarily suspended or canceled their orders from the suppliers – often based in South, Southeast, and East Asia.

Second, the vulnerability of suppliers to such sudden changes in demand appeared to be an inherent feature of their participation in GVCs. Hence, local "boom and bust economies," of which suppliers in the Global South formed part, appeared to highlight the inherent short-term benefits that may be derived from participation in such chains, but also the risk of such local economies experiencing "inmiserizing growth" in which local exports and jobs expand in the short run but are followed by a long-term decline in living standards (Kaplinsky, 2005).

Third, the outbreak of COVID-19 in the early parts of 2020 seemed to reinforce the idea that workers laboring at the base of GVCs are inherently vulnerable to sudden changes in global demand. During periods of economic expansion, these workers may be incorporated into the global economy by entering into low-paid jobs in labor-intensive, low-skilled occupations. This may be associated with a short-term increase in their earnings, compared to what they might be able to earn in domestic value chains or being un or under-employed. It also comes with the risk of workers being compelled to doing excessive overtime, facing severe occupational health, safety, and fire risks, as observed at the time of the collapse of the Rana Plaza building in Bangladesh in 2013.

In other words, the outbreak of COVID-19 seemed to be an opportune moment to reflect on what we have learned about the possibility of managing buyers, suppliers, and workers in socially responsible ways in GVCs that link countries in the Global North with producer nations in the Global South. In fact, my research in the last fifteen years has concentrated on investigating corporate social responsibility (CSR) in these chains through studies in the leather tanning industry in Pakistan (2005–2007), the football manufacturing industries of China, India, and Pakistan (2007–2012), multi-stakeholder initiatives (the Better Cotton Initiative in particular) in the garment and textiles industries of India and Pakistan, and most recently the bamboo value chains of India (2019–2021). Throughout the last fifteen years of research into CSR in GVCs I have conducted (or been part of research teams that undertook) approximately 900 interviews with buyers in North America and Europe, suppliers, subcontractors, workers, farmers, international organizations, national government representatives, NGOs, trade unions, and other actors. Hence, the invitation from Edward Elgar and the outbreak of COVID-19 seemed to be a useful opportunity to rethink and reassess what we know about CSR in GVCs based on the many studies and my own work carried out in this field since 2005.

At the outset, I should also emphasize that I do not attempt to empirically document and analyze current and ongoing events during the COVID-19 pandemic. In my view, a longer time frame is required to understand these dramatic and unfolding events, and, as Neil Coe argues in his recent (2021) book, these changes in GVC organization are likely to keep scholars in this field busy for the next ten years. Moreover, the implications of COVID-19 for CSR in GVCs is likely to vary across industries, value chains, producer countries, and importing countries. Hence, dissecting the long-term consequences of COVID-19 for CSR in GVCs will require more narrowly focused studies that take into account these variations – a task that is beyond the scope of the current book.

Instead, I use short stories/examples/quotations from buyers/suppliers/ workers affected by COVID-19 as caveats to introduce some of the broader theoretical and empirical challenges that have been confronting a variety of value chain actors since I first started studying CSR in GVCs fifteen years ago. In analyzing how CSR has been incorporated and strategically integrated in GVCs in the last fifteen years, I am still astounded by how often actors in the Global North including brands, NGOs, trade unions, and government officials tend to "forget" or underestimate just how much inequality is entrenched in the very structuring of these chains (see also McCarthy and Moon, 2018).

For instance, the purchasing practices of major brands sourcing garments from a country such as Bangladesh tend to result in downward price pressures, seasonal fluctuations in demand, and shorter lead times while, at the same time, these brands are also imposing ever greater environmental and labor standard requirements on their suppliers (not only in Bangladesh but elsewhere in the Global South). Economic value is very unevenly distributed along the textile/garment value chain, with major brands reaping up to ten times higher economic value than suppliers – and even less reaching workers. In this context, local suppliers have few incentives to engage in CSR as defined by their buyers in Europe and North America.

In fact, I keep reflecting on how challenging it is for brands, suppliers, and workers to align their interests in GVC participation in ways that might ultimately benefit workers at the base of the chain. Hence, a large part of my scholarly engagement in the last fifteen years has concentrated on identifying the circumstances under which it might actually be possible to find a "sweet spot" in CSR in GVCs so that value chain participation could be mutually beneficial for brands, suppliers, and workers instead of winding up with the repeated conclusion, "it can't be done," as some studies in this field sometimes appear to assume.

However, apart from the inherent inequality in GVCs, I also find that the last fifteen years of empirically based work on CSR in GVCs has emphasized a repeated failure of brands, NGOs, government officials, and other actors in the Global North to listen and address the valid CSR concerns of suppliers and workers in the Global South (see also, Van der Ven et al., 2021). This point was powerfully illustrated in a recent conference video for the 2021 OECD Forum on Due Diligence in the Garment and Footwear Sector. Here the President of the Bangladesh garments and exporters association (BGMEA), Rubana Huq, stated,

> We live in different worlds. We live in one where regulations are handed over to us [i.e. the Global South], and the other world is of course the world that regulates [i.e., the Global North]. The point is that there is a distinct disconnect between what is being given to us, and what we are understanding, and are we aware of what is being given to us? Are we aligned with the expectations? And how are we going to be ever able to comply with any of them, apart from just ticking the boxes, if we are not actually consulted in the process of assessment?

> So if you really want a level playing field, then all the worlds, basically both the worlds, need to converge, and we must be broadly inclusive in all the stakeholder dialogues, and while a legislation is being framed [i.e., on human rights and environmental due diligence in the EU], it is imperative that the countries who are expected to comply must be taken into consideration. A multi-stakeholder based, all inclusive, consultative process is required so that no country ever feels being left out in the process. (Huq, 2021)

What this quote from Dr. Rubana Huq powerfully illustrates is that it is hard to imagine any kind of progress being made on CSR in GVCs if only the perspectives of Global North actors regarding CSR are taken into account and then "exported" throughout GVCs in the expectation that factories and workers will automatically comply with or share these views of CSR. An important intellectual task in this book is therefore to identify, compare, and contrast the different assumptions, views, and perceptions of CSR amongst brands, suppliers, and workers that it has been possible to identify through the last fifteen years of empirical work on this issue. And then try to see whether there is any way of bridging these views, in ways that allow for more meaningful, inclusive action to take place on social responsibility issues in ways that allow for mutual financial and social benefits being shared along the GVC, rather than suppliers, and especially workers, having to bear the costs of value chain participation.

I first started conducting detailed empirical studies in this field fifteen years ago. My aim here is to create a more complete account of what we know, what we don't, and what we need to know about CSR in GVCs that seeks to integrate mainly theoretical, and to a lesser extent empirical, insights into this field. In doing so, I draw upon our earlier collaborative work and the insights of many colleagues who have helped shape my thinking on this subject. In the introductory chapter, the analytical framework presented draws extensively on my earlier collaboration with Adam Lindgreen in our 2018 article on the sweet spot in ethical trade in *Geoforum*. In Chapter 2, I employ key discussions and insights from an earlier working paper elaborated with my CBS colleague, Jacobo Ramirez, on rethinking CSR in GVCs in the age of COVID-19. Chapter 3 draws upon my recent paper on supplier perspectives on CSR in GVCs published in *Environment and Planning A* in 2020. Chapter 4 on cluster perspectives on CSR and GVCs has extensively benefitted from earlier discussions and feedback on various drafts of the chapter from Lauren McCarthy, Zartashia Ahmed, and Alex Hughes. Chapter 5 is an update of my earlier article on labor agency in GVCs elaborated together with Neil Coe and published in the *Journal of Economic Geography* in 2015. Along with these colleagues I would like to thank my mentor and friend Khalid Nadvi as well as Gary Gereffi, Stephanie Barrientos, and Stefano Ponte for their continued constructive feedback, support, and encouragement in relation to developing my work. And my wife, Uzma Rehman, for her love, support, and always helping me finding the right balance between outer and inner work in this life.

As I argue in this book, writings on CSR in GVCs in the last fifteen years have come from a variety of angles and perspectives. I use this book as an opportunity for creating a more integrated and elaborate perspective on the contestation of CSR in the interaction between buyers, suppliers, and workers in GVCs, critically examining the potential for finding a sweet spot in which the interests of these actors intersect.

1. Introduction: rethinking global value chains and corporate social responsibility

INTRODUCTION

In 2020, COVID-19 was associated with a major shake-up of global value chains (GVCs) connecting consumers, brands, and retailers in the Global North with local producers, workers, and communities in the Global South (Gereffi, 2020). Initially, in January and February 2020, COVID-19 hit China, leading to a temporary closure of large parts of the "world's factory floor" as thousands of factories either had to slow production or close. When COVID-19 reached North America and Europe in March and April of 2020, country-wide lock-downs and closure of retail outlets led to a dramatic fall in the international demand for products such as clothes and shoes (Rankin, 2020).

The knock-on effect could quickly be seen in many producer countries where factory closures and job losses were acutely felt (Leitheiser et al., 2020). For instance, in Bangladesh, hundreds of thousands of workers faced an abrupt loss of income, possibly leading to the starvation of their families, as their factory owners were not receiving payments for orders already shipped or faced sudden cancellation of orders from their buyers in the Global North (Anner, 2020). In India, millions of migrant workers were suddenly on the move as the workplaces shut down. Without possible alternative sources of income, they were struggling to travel hundreds, if not thousands of miles on foot, to their native villages at a time when nation-wide transport had been shut down (BBC News, 2020). In addition, with a sudden dramatic world-wide increase in the demand for hand sanitizers and safety masks, workers in some factories in the Global South had to work around the clock to help their employers accelerate production (Gereffi, 2020). All the while these workers suddenly had to be trained in physical distancing and other safety measures at the factory premises (Channel 4, 2020). At the same time, suppliers sometimes introduced new, discriminatory hiring practices. For instance, in Mexico, new job postings sometimes required that workers should not have any diseases including hypertension, diabetes, or obesity which could put them at risk during COVID-19 (Casaola, 2020).

In many ways, these dramatic events of the first six months of 2020 highlighted some of the systemic issues that have continued to plague the world of CSR in GVCs for the last twenty years. It is therefore an opportune moment to reflect upon what we learned about the theory and practice of CSR in GVCs since the turn of the millennium, and this book is dedicated to achieving this intellectual tasks. Inspired by Blowfield and Frynas (2005), I adopt a rather broad definition of CSR in this book. I thus see CSR as a process through which companies attempt to address the social and environmental effects of their business operations, make sure that their business partners operate in ethical ways, manage their stakeholder relations, and seek to achieve wider social legitimacy. However, later in the book, I will return to unpacking the multiple, contested interpretations of CSR in GVCs.

WHY WRITE A BOOK ON CSR IN GVCS?

As I explained in the preface, events associated with the eruption of COVID-19 highlighted some of the challenging aspects of buyer (ir)responsibility towards the thousands of suppliers and workers that depend upon their participation in GVCs as a way of sustaining job creation, maintain "decent" work conditions, and social protection of workers. An important motivation for writing this book is thus my long-standing interest in untangling current, dominating buyer-centered perspectives on CSR in GVCs, examine their main strengths and limitations, and consider whether we need to rethink (or completely discard) these buyer-centric approaches to CSR in GVCs in order to create a more long-term sustainable outcome for local factories and workers in the Global South.

At the same time, the rapid disruption and temporary restructuring of GVCs during the initial phases of COVID-19 in early 2020 highlighted some of the challenges facing suppliers in relation to CSR in GVCs. In the context of the global garments industry, interrelated processes such as the transition to neoliberalism in the North, the phase-out of quotas in the South, the depression of export prices, and an escalation of non-price requirements created a "supplier squeeze" (see also Ponte, 2019). This supplier squeeze incentivizes manufacturers to push worker wages below reproduction costs and/or make workers labor to the point where they are beyond exhaustion (Marslev, 2020). These supplier squeezes also created what has been described as the "factory manager's dilemmas" (Khan et al., 2020). This concept seeks to capture how the purchasing practices of lead firms – promoted by their sourcing departments – often means that brands squeeze product prices and demands for quick adaptation due to sudden or seasonal changes in demand. In this way, last minute orders can lead to lower wages, short-term and casual contracts and excessive overtime work, prompting local factory managers to cut corners when it comes to managing their workforce in a socially responsible way. At the same time, the sustainability/CSR departments of lead firms may require suppliers to increase worker wages, provide longer-term contracts and social insurance as well as labor codes of conduct/certifications. In short, this means that enhanced CSR performance of suppliers cannot be meaningfully expected without considering the importance of suppliers' financial viability. In light of COVID-19, we can also extend this line of argument by noting that the factory managers' dilemma also extends to how they should handle CSR in GVCs during a sudden disruption of their value chains with a view to maintaining job and income security for their workers, manage "responsible" temporary lay-offs of their employees, and unemployment and/or pension insurance of workers.

Hence, my second motivation for writing this book is my long-term interest in advancing a supplier-centered perspective on CSR in GVCs, trying to understand the diversity of interests and CSR perceptions of suppliers across a variety of contexts in the Global South. My interest in pursuing this line of inquiry also stems from the constant assumption amongst some brands, NGOs, trade union practitioners, and students as well as government officials in Europe that CSR is something that is mainly defined by corporations in Europe and North America and then "exported" through GVCs to "irresponsible suppliers" in the Global South. In my view, such views often stem from a lack of critical self-reflection – both in relation to understanding how importers in Europe and North America – through their purchasing practices – play an important part of creating sub-standard work conditions in some export-oriented companies in the Global South. Moreover, such views may also have to do with the relative ignorance, or rather ignoring, of pre-existing supplier-centered views of CSR that must be acknowledged and incorporated into existing CSR approaches of the so-called "global brands" if CSR improvements are to be more long-term and sustainable in the Global South.

Finally, to me, the events in early 2020 also raised both questions and concerns about how workers can defend their interests in GVCs, and the extent to which they can strategically make use of CSR in GVCs towards this end. Often buyer-centric approaches (and to some extent also supplier-centered approaches) to CSR in GVCs tend to overlook the agency of workers themselves to strategically use CSR to hold brands and suppliers responsible for their actions, using this as a lever to improve their own working conditions at the base of GVCs. Hence, in my view, labor agency in relation to CSR in GVCs can both be constituted through formal and informal means. Formal labor agency here refers to how workers can defend their interests in GVCs through trade unions by engaging in collective bargaining and having freedom of association. Informal labor agency has to do with the informal actions of workers through which they may opt in and out of work forms and workplaces in line with their broader interests and life circumstances. Here CSR may be important to the extent that workers, by their own choice, decide to seek jobs in work forms/workplaces that – in their own understanding may have more socially responsible approaches towards the management of their own workforce. Hence, labor agency may both be conceived as a continuum from worker action in the formal economy to worker mobilizing in the informal economy, and it also needs to be considered across various scales, from local to national, regional and international levels.

Moreover, in the light of recent events with disruptions of GVCs in early 2020, it seems as if buyers, workers, and suppliers in GVCs may not only have contrasting (and often contradictory) interests in CSR in GVCs, but that it may also be highly challenging to reconcile these interests. Not only due to the fluidity and changing nature of GVCs but also perhaps because buyer, supplier, and worker perceptions of what constitutes socially responsible behavior may be highly different. Hence, in intellectual terms, I am interested in analytically teasing out the circumstances under which it may be possible to identify a sweet spot – or a point in which buyer, supplier, and worker interests in CSR might intersect, and where it may be possible to bridge what otherwise appear to be irreconcilable interests in CSR in GVCs.

Finally, in what some commentators have described as "building back better," the dramatic events of early 2020 have made it apparent that there is a need to consider how we go forward from here if we are not only to achieve a greater intellectual understanding and insights into CSR in GVCs but also secure a fairer distribution of economic and social gains and risks associated with participation of buyers, suppliers, and workers in GVCs. In many ways, some of these broader issues require a more in-depth consideration which is beyond the scope of this book. However, in looking back at what we have learned – both theoretically and empirically – about CSR in GVCs in the last twenty years, I also wish to establish both a future research and policy agenda for the next decade on CSR in GVCs. In my view, this will require that we pay greater attention to issues such as international regulation (human rights due diligence in particular), building more circular economy models in GVCs, and addressing the need for climate mitigation/adaptation as we move towards 2030.

In the rest of the introduction to this book, I will first elaborate on my understanding of CSR in GVCs as both having a relational and contextual connotation. I then go into introducing the main research questions that the book seeks to address before I outline what I consider an integrated view of buyer-, supplier-, and worker-centered perceptions of CSR in GVCs that serves as a basic structuring for the rest of the book, as it seeks to critically examine what we have learned about CSR in GVCs in the last twenty years from the perspectives of buyers, suppliers, and workers. Finally, the introduction contains a short discussion of the contents of the individual book chapters and the conclusion.

DEFINING CSR IN THE CONTEXT OF GLOBAL VALUE CHAINS

In this book, I see CSR as both relational and contested. Following D'Cruz et al. (2021), I perceive CSR as:

> A relational view of negotiating, organizing and implementing responsibilities towards economic, social, technological and environmental issues across organizations/workplaces, groups and individuals. Thus we see social responsibilities as being in flux, determined by negotiated roles and associated expectations that individuals, groups and organizations/workplaces construct and adopt in relation to other actors. We frame social responsibilities as the division of labor and accountability between and among actors in a particular context embedded within the associated structural conditions, when aiming at some wider societal good.

Adopting this relational view of CSR, I zoom in on the perspectives of three central actors typically involved in CSR in GVCs: brands, suppliers, and workers at the base of these chains (Lund-Thomsen and Lindgreen, 2018). My focus on these actors is justified by the fact that they are the ones that have typically been at the core of "ethical trade." Following the United Kingdom Ethical Trade Initiative the director of (UK-ETI) (2017), I take ethical trade to mean that retailers, brands, and their suppliers take responsibility for improving the working conditions of the people who make the products they sell. In the context of COVID-19, the UK-ETI (2021) thus states, "as the coronavirus pandemic continues to unfold, disrupting supply chains and impacting workers on an unprecedented global scale, I have adjusted our operations to optimize support for the forward-thinking companies, trade unions, and NGOs that make up our members."

In this book, I also adopt a view of CSR as highly contextualized. As D'Cruz and her colleagues argue, CSR is governed through a range of institutions at the national level, including states, markets, corporations, professional organizations, NGOs, trade unions, and communities, and also broader institutions such as multi-stakeholder initiatives and public–private partnerships (Amaeshi and Idemudia, 2015; Motsei and Nkomo, 2016) and 'new' institutions such as multi-stakeholder initiatives and public–private partnerships (Ponte, 2019; Riisgaard et al., 2020). As such, CSR is practiced by a variety of organizations and workplaces in society, but these interact with wider systems of governance and are constantly subject to negotiation and resistance (D'Cruz et al., 2021).

Paraphrasing Neilson and Pritchard (2009), we can thus say that CSR must be understood as highly contested and negotiated through the interaction of vertical relations (the interactions between buyers, suppliers, and workers) and highly diverse institutional contexts, resulting in what these authors call "value chain struggles" over the economic, social, and environmental conditions under which products and services are to be produced in export-oriented industries in the Global South.

MAIN CONTRIBUTIONS

This book departs from earlier writings on CSR in GVCs that address diverse topics such as the gendered nature of CSR (McCarthy, 2017; McCarthy and Moon, 2018) and the strategic use of CSR by social movements to promote workers' rights in GVCs (Bair and Palpacuer, 2015), Some authors in this literature have also investigated whether CSR can help promote labor and human rights in industrial clusters that are tied into GVCs (Gereffi and Lee, 2016; Giuliani, 2016). Furthermore, scholarly interest has zoomed in on the impacts of corporate codes of conduct and buyer purchasing practices on workers' conditions (Bartley and Egels-Zandén, 2015; Bartley, 2018, Anner, 2020). In addition, several authors have analyzed divergent buyer and supplier perspectives on CSR in GVCs (Lund-Thomsen and Lindgreen, 2018; Asif et al., 2019; Perry et al., 2015; Lund-Thomsen, 2020) and whether CSR enhances or undermines labor agency in such chains (Lund-Thomsen and Coe, 2015; Kumar, 2019). However, whereas there is a now an embryonic literature on the implications of COVID-19 on GVCs (Carmody, 2020; Gereffi, 2020; Morton, 2020), there is still – in my view – a gap in the literature, which this book tries to fill, when it comes to making a more comprehensive critical appreciation of the circumstances in which buyer, supplier, and worker perspectives on CSR in GVCs (do not) intersect in the light of COVID-19. In other words, there is a space for a monograph that looks back at the last 15 years of theorizing and empirical work on CSR in GVCs with a view to building back better, as we – at the time of writing – are still in the midst of COVID-19 and hopefully will soon move beyond its immediate effects. This book is an initial attempt at filling part of this gap in our knowledge.

KEY RESEARCH QUESTIONS

My core research question is thus: *In which circumstances is it possible to identify a sweet spot in CSR in GVCs where the interests of buyers, suppliers, and workers in GVCs intersect?*

I break this main question down into three sub-questions:

a.   What are the drivers, main features, conceptual underpinnings, and limitations of the buyer-driven compliance and cooperation paradigms to CSR in GVCs?

b.   Why are suppliers in the Global South that are integrated into GVCs often highly skeptical of CSR?

c.   In which circumstances may the CSR policies of internationally branded companies facilitate or undermine worker agency at the level of supplier factories?

THE ANALYTICAL FRAMEWORK OF THE BOOK

In order to theorize how CSR has been interpreted, negotiated, and adjusted in the interaction between buyers, suppliers, and workers, I set out the theoretical framework of the book in the next part of the introduction. In turn, I take the perspectives of three central actors typically involved in CSR in GVCs: buyers/brands, suppliers in the Global South, and workers at the base of these chains (Lund-Thomsen and Lindgreen, 2018). By applying all three perspectives, I theorize about the circumstances in which CSR might contribute to an optimal situation in which buyer, supplier, and worker interests intersect in a sweet spot, reflecting an amended version of Gereffi et al.'s (2005) theory of value chain governance.

I critically appraise the potential and limitations of CSR to achieve this aim and highlight the need to consider three key factors: (1) the type of GVCs that buyers, suppliers, and workers pursue (i.e., ranging from market-based transactions to hierarchy); (2) the national context of work and employment in which GVCs function; and (3) the perspectives expressed by buyers, suppliers, and workers in relation to make buyer, supplier, and worker interests converge. A resulting matrix contains 12 possible instances in which we can identify this combination of factors (or their absence) in relation to making CSR achieve this aim. Accordingly, I show that not all circumstances are sufficient to achieve such a convergence. However, instead of simply dismissing the possibility altogether, I contend that its identification becomes more feasible as we move from market-based transactions towards hierarchical GVCs, though its establishment is also very context dependent. At the intersection of vertical relations (interfirm relations) and horizontal relations (national context of work and employment), the joint interests of buyers, suppliers, and workers in addressing the negative impacts of COVID-19 on working conditions in the industry can be created or undermined within GVCs.

In the next section, I introduce the GVC approach, which serves as a theoretical frame for my analysis of buyer, supplier, and worker perspectives on CSR. Then I offer a critical appraisal of the potential for and limitations to finding a sweet spot, according to these three viewpoints. To establish a conceptual map of the circumstances in which it may (not) be possible to identify a point at which the interests of buyers, suppliers, and workers intersect, I articulate an amended version of Gereffi et al.'s (2005) theory of value chain governance.

THE GLOBAL VALUE CHAIN APPROACH

I here define GVCs as "the full range of activities that firms, farmers and workers carry out to bring a product or service from its conception to its end use, recycling or reuse. These activities include design, production, processing, assembly, distribution, maintenance and repair, disposal/recycling, marketing, finance and consumer services. In a GVC, these functions are distributed among many firms scattered around the world" (Ponte et al., 2019, p. 1). GVCs extend beyond interfirm relationships in value or commodity chains to involve a wide range of actors: states, nongovernmental organizations (NGOs), trade unions, social movements, and other relevant entities that shape the conditions surrounding interfirm linkages in the global economy. They are inherently dynamic and in flux, in the processes of becoming, changing, and alternating. Some GVCs are short-lived, but others persist; some are relatively localized, whereas others span several continents. Thus, GVCs are multi-scalar and feature international, regional, national, provincial, and local levels (Coe and Yeung, 2015a).

They also have strong institutional features, such that GVCs are "quite literally grounded in specific locations. Such grounding is both material (the fixed assets of production), and also less tangible (localized social relationships and distinctive institutions and cultural practices)" (Coe et al., 2008, p. 279). This concept of embeddedness is central, though we must distinguish between territorial embeddedness (i.e., geographical places) and network embeddedness (i.e., connections among network participants, regardless of geographical position). Furthermore, GVCs are embedded in spatial and social arrangements that influence GVC actors' strategies, including the "values, priorities, and expectations of managers, workers, and communities alike" (Henderson et al., 2002, p. 451).

In turn, participating firms, governments, workers, and other actors all have distinct priorities with regard to profitability, growth, and economic development (Lund-Thomsen and Lindgreen, 2014). Debates about which norms and values should guide the governance of GVCs constitute value chain struggles (Neilson and Pritchard, 2009, 2010), which suggests that GVCs also are contested fields "in which actors struggle over the construction of economic relationships, governance structures, institutional rules and norms, and discursive frames" (Levy, 2008, p. 944). The resulting power relations in GVCs are neither unidirectional nor structurally determined; they involve both "cooperation and collaboration" and "conflict and competition" across the actors, brands, suppliers, and workers (Coe et al., 2008). Moreover, the outcomes of value chain struggles are determined jointly by vertical and horizontal network relations. The former refer to power relations between buyers and suppliers in GVCs; the latter reflect the influences of different institutional levels, from economic, labor, and environmental laws to the informal norms embraced by private-sector firms, international organizations, trade unions, or NGOs, all of which operate at various geographical scales (Lund-Thomsen and Coe, 2015; Neilson and Pritchard, 2010).

This outline of the basic contours of the GVC approach provides a central organizing device for critically appraising the prospects for and hindrances to finding an optimum point in CSR, from the perspectives of buyers, suppliers, and workers from which their interests can be bridged during a global economic slowdown such as COVID-19. I start the analysis with the buyer perspective.

Buyer Perspectives

If we look at CSR literature from the perspective of international buyers, two dominant approaches emerge that offer very different implications for the notion of finding a common point at which the interests of buyers, suppliers, and workers intersect (Locke, 2013). The first refers to a *compliance model* or strategy, in which buyers develop a code of conduct, require first-tier suppliers to abide by this code, monitor whether it is being implemented (e.g., first-, second-, or third-party auditing), develop a plan for remediating any code violations, and ultimately cut ties with suppliers that are non-compliant (Locke et al., 2009). The second, *commitment approach* (Locke et al., 2009) entails a collaborative model to social upgrading in GVCs (Locke and Romis, 2010).[1]

The compliance-based model has been widely criticized for failing to align the interests of buyers, suppliers, and workers in CSR (Lund-Thomsen and Lindgreen, 2014). In this model, retailers mainly pursue their own interests, seeking to avoid negative publicity and damage to their brand value due to media exposures of poor working conditions at the base of their GVCs. Instead of assisting their suppliers in improving compliance levels, international buyers engage in the unilateral extraction of compliance-related information from suppliers, which they then use as evidence to convince national regulators, NGOs, and the media that they are in control of the work conditions at the base of their GVCs (Lund-Thomsen, 2008). Costs simply get added to the supplier production processes, through the imposition of top-down, bureaucratic auditing and control procedures that do little to improve the quality or quantity of work available in these factories. In a sense, a compliance-based approach actively undermines the potential for identifying a point at which the interests of buyers, suppliers, and workers intersect in CSR – particularly when buyers grant suppliers perverse incentives to "keep up appearances" or engage in unethical employee coaching or auditing fraud instead of genuinely taking responsibility for work conditions in their GVCs (Lund-Thomsen and Lindgreen, 2014).

From the buyer's perspective, the cooperative approach seems to offer better prospects for finding a sweet spot in CSR where the interests of buyers, suppliers, and workers can be aligned in ameliorating the negative impacts of COVID-19 on the conditions of garment workers at the base of these chains (Lund-Thomsen and Ramirez, 2020). With this approach, buyers help suppliers by redesigning their sourcing practices and rewarding suppliers that abide by their codes of conduct, offering more business or better prices for the products they produce. Furthermore, buyers seek to align their own interests with those of suppliers and workers by maintaining long-term business rela-tionships with first-tier suppliers and engaging in capacity-building programs to improve the work organization, worker productivity, and labor conditions in factory settings (Distelhorst et al., 2016).

Although the cooperative approach thus appears to represent a "genuine" attempt to identify joint buyer, supplier, and worker interests, little hard evidence supports the main assertions underlying its predicted benefits. To the extent that evidence exists, it is anecdotal; for example, Distelhorst et al. (2016), in a study of more than 300 Nike suppliers, find that Nike's intensive training in lean manufacturing principles led to a 15% reduction in serious labor rights violations, but there were no discernible effects on health, safety, or environmental performance. Hoffman et al. (2014) similarly find that a col-laborative approach involving capacity building, employee-controlled worker committees, and a confidential worker's hotline enabled Chinese workers to voice their concerns, which led to enhanced worker satisfaction and reduced overtime. Yet in their study of Hewlett-Packard's supplier responsibility program, Distelhorst et al. (2015) argue instead that national contexts – not supply chain power, repeated audits, or capability building – best explain differences in workplace social compliance levels. In their study, factories in China tended to be less compliant than suppliers in other countries that had stronger civil society and regulatory institutions, for example.

In short, there is little to indicate that a compliance-based approach is helpful for finding an optimum point in CSR. The cooperative approach appears to offer better opportunities for finding such a point. Yet, if we take the perspective of buyers in isolation, it thus appears uncertain whether there are any real prospects of finding a sweet spot in CSR.

Supplier Perspectives

Suppliers in GVCs vary in their size, the products they produce, the industries in which they operate, and their geographical spread. I therefore address how such diversity might affect the prospects of identifying a sweet spot where their interests align with buyers and workers in mitigating the negative impacts of COVID-19 on workers at the base of GVCs.

Before doing so though, I note some relevant, common, cross-cutting themes in prior literature devoted to supplier perspectives. First, suppliers in different industries – garments, football, and footwear manufacturing for example – often locate in specific but diverse locations (e.g., Pakistan, India, Vietnam, Indonesia, China; Gereffi and Lee, 2016; Nadvi, 2014). Thus, manufacturing sites frequently supply the same kind of products, of similar quality, leading suppliers in different countries to compete with one another, in a downward spiral of price competition (Lund-Thomsen et al., 2012). This situation places some structural limitations on the extent to which suppliers can align their interests with those of buyers and workers in CSR. Second, unit prices have tended to decline over time in different industries, even as the cost of raw materials frequently has increased. With profitability being razor thin, there are fewer financial benefits available for suppliers to share with workers (Hobbes, 2015). Third, seasonal demand for items such as clothing and footballs means that suppliers must adjust their production capacity accordingly, causing instability in the availability of jobs and worker incomes. Fourth, lead times have tended to decrease over time, particularly in the fast fashion segment, so suppliers face simultaneous demands for better quality, lower prices, and ever-shorter lead times, which frequently require workers to engage in overtime work. Here again, I observe that the CSR interests of suppliers and workers appear pitched against each other (Tokatli et al., 2008).

Turning to how the diversity of suppliers in the Global South affects the prospects for identifying an optimum point in CSR, I note that *supplier size* appears to be a key factor. Giant contractors from countries such as Hong Kong, China, South Korea, and Taiwan are widespread in the garment and electronics industries (Knorringa and Nadvi, 2016). For example, the Hong Kong-based Li and Fung and Taiwan-based Foxconn own or source from thousands of factories throughout Asia, Latin America, and Africa.[2] These giant contractors also tend to run modern, well-equipped factories that offer higher wages and more regulated work environments than are available in informal jobs. They are also in a much stronger bargaining position in the value chain than smaller-scale suppliers. The workforces in Asian-owned factories tend to consist of young, low-wage, female workers who are housed in dormitories at the production site (Appelbaum, 2008). For these large-scale suppliers, it likely is easier to achieve economies of scale and higher levels of productivity that – at least in theory – could enable them to align their interests with brands' and workers' (Lund-Thomsen et al., 2012).

However, the same cannot be said for the prospects of small to medium-sized enterprises (SMEs). Because SMEs often lack the capital, infrastructure, knowledge, and human resources required to achieve economies of scale and high levels of productivity, it might be more challenging for them to align their interests with those of brands and workers (Jamali et al., 2017). They might take informal steps towards aligning their interests with those of their workers though. Such efforts typically include community donations, providing workers with tea, or paying the bills for their workers' children's weddings (Sachdeva and Panfil, 2008). However, from a buyer perspective, such practices do not resonate with either the compliance or the cooperation approaches, which mainly recognize formal improvements to work conditions (e.g., minimum wages, being paid for overtime, access to social insurance). Therefore, for SMEs, finding the sweet spot in CSR is particularly challenging.[3]

In addition to company size, finding this optimum point depends on the end market into which producers sell, from a supplier perspective (Barrientos et al., 2016). CSR literature typically conceives of "vertical" world trade as taking place between buyers in North America or Europe and suppliers in the Global South. However, recent findings indicate the ever-growing importance of horizontal trade between buyers and suppliers throughout the Global South. Part of this trade stems from the growing exchange of intermediary components across countries in the Global South, with the final products still being sold in the Global North (Horner and Nadvi, 2018). However, a fundamental horizontal shift in global trade also has arisen for products that are both manufactured and sold in the growing home markets of countries such as India and China (Horner, 2016). From the viewpoint of suppliers, shifting trade trends have several pertinent implications for identifying CSR areas in which they share interests with buyers and workers.

First, suppliers engaging in horizontal trade might not be as interested in CSR. As the importance of local and regional value production networks grows, due to increasing domestic demand in countries such as China, India, and Brazil (Knorringa and Nadvi, 2016), their participation in CSR – in a traditional sense, such that suppliers in developing countries seek to sell their products to buyers in Northern markets – may become less attractive for suppliers in the Global South. Second, even if suppliers in the Global South can access more local, regional, and global alternatives for selling their products to end buyers, they still likely face standard social and environmental pressures in their domestic contexts (Pickles et al., 2016). In particular, "Southern standards" have begun to proliferate in developing countries and economies in transition, focused mainly on obtaining producer buy-in and targeting consumer audiences within these countries. To some extent, these standards also seek to address local implementation gaps and distance themselves, in both cognitive and moral terms, from existing Western standards (Schouten and Bitzer, 2015). Whether such emerging standards also translate into the identification of an optimal point that aligns the interests of buyers, suppliers, and workers in the Global South remains an empirical question.

In summary, suppliers in the Global South face a range of structural constraints that may prevent them from identifying common interests with buyers and suppliers in CSR. Moreover, the prospects for identifying such joint interests vary, across suppliers of different sizes and among suppliers that serve different end markets. In turn, this is also related to the horizontal dimension of value chain analysis, as suppliers operate within different national regulatory contexts, are supported by various upgrading initiatives in particular industries, and face different production cost structures that – in part – depend upon worker wage levels in different countries.

Worker Perspectives

In my analysis of buyer and supplier perspectives, I mainly address their vertical relations. However, many of the factors reflected in the supplier perspective also influence the prospects of workers, in terms of whether they can identify common CSR interests with brands and suppliers. If suppliers earn lower unit rates over time, workers also tend to receive lower wages. If suppliers must reduce lead times, workers will have to engage in overtime work. Thus, the optimum point for suppliers and workers is inherently linked.

To address worker perspectives, I also turn to the importance of horizontal relations though, as reflected in the national and institutional context that surrounds work and employment (Carswell and De Neve, 2013). I posit that worker perspectives on the optimal point in CSR are mediated by the specific socio-economic and socio-cultural contexts in which they are embedded (Coe and Jordhus-Lier, 2011; Sportel, 2013; Tran and Jeppesen, 2016). In terms of structure, these contexts may facilitate or undermine the possibilities that workers have for aligning their interests with suppliers' and buyers'. For example, in the Sri Lankan garment industry, the country's active labor movement and proliferation of labor laws, particularly in its pre-independence period, likely provided the initial space for formal labor organizing (Ruwanpura, 2015). However, in the post-liberalization period after 1977, this space shrunk, and unions have had difficulty organizing the labor force, because they fail to take the gendered, cultured, and spatial particularities of working lives in Sri Lanka into account (Ruwanpura, 2016). In a very different setting, Chan (2014) argues that Chinese garment workers have begun to challenge the regulatory framework established by the state. However, the pre-occupation of Chinese authorities, particularly at the provincial level, with attracting foreign direct investment appears to promote a capital over a labor policy, and the state's manipulation of trade unions limits workers' ability to organize collectively in an efficient way. In other words, in terms of horizontal relations, national and regional economic and labor legislation, as well as the enforcement agencies of the state, constitute important determinants of the structural space within which workers might align their interests with buyers' and suppliers'.

An additional factor to consider is the availability of cheap, surplus, often female rural labor that has been present in countries such as China, Vietnam, and Cambodia during parts of their industrialization (Marslev, 2020). The greater the availability of such labor, the more difficult it will be for workers to negotiate improvements in their wages and work conditions. Nevertheless, I would still argue that the more progressive economic and labor legislation and enforcement is, in terms of protecting the interests of workers in CSR, the greater the scope for them to reap the potential benefits of taking part in such trade.

Yet workers' options for aligning their interests with buyers' and suppliers' in CSR are not determined solely by the structural space. A rich literature documents the ways in which workers exercise labor agency to determine their own conditions at work at the base of GVCs (Alford et al., 2017; Coe and Hess, 2013; Coe and Jordhus-Lier, 2011; Lund-Thomsen and Coe, 2015; Ruwanpura, 2015). I define labor agency as workers acting either collectively to defend their interests through trade unions or informally by opting in or out of particular workplaces and work forms, depending on their personal preferences and broader life circumstances (Carswell and De Neve, 2013). In the Sialkot football manufacturing cluster, Lund-Thomsen (2013) observes that the possibilities of workers to exercise labor agency relates to the diversity of livelihood strategies pursued by football stitchers, and the spatial location of these stitchers in relation to more centralized workplaces may constrain their ability to opt in and out of factory-based, stitching center, and home-based work locations. In other words, their ability to insert themselves into GVCs in ways where workers, and not only brands and suppliers, benefit from taking part in CSR may be limited.

Moreover, the possibilities for workers to identify a sweet spot in CSR can be highly gendered, in the sense that female workers are more pressed to find ways to combine childcare and household chores with full-time work in centralized factory settings. Even if it would be financially profitable for these workers to engage in formal factory-based work, it may be incompatible with their broader responsibilities in the reproductive economy. Accordingly, De Neve (2014) notes that young, unmarried, female migrant workers appear to prefer working full-time in a formalized factory setting in the Tiruppur garment cluster, where they also have access to housing facilities. However, in the Jalandhar football cluster, Khara and Lund-Thomsen (2012) find that older stitchers, both male and female, work in home-based settings that grant them greater flexibility in terms of the pace with which they hand stich the products. Finding an optimum point in CSR, from the perspective of workers, thus may be a highly gendered process that also depends on factors such as workers' life cycles, broader family relations, and positioning within local communities.

Having outlined the buyer, supplier, and worker perspectives, in the next section I return to a foundational research question: In which circumstances is it possible to identify a sweet spot in CSR?

TOWARDS AN INTEGRATED ANALYTICAL MODEL

To identify circumstances in which buyer, supplier, and worker interests in CSR overlap, I refer to three factors: (1) vertical relations, reflecting the nature of the interactions among buyers, first-tier suppliers, and their workers in GVCs; (2) the particular perspectives that each actor (buyer, supplier, and workers) in these relationships have on CSR in GVCs; and (3) horizontal relations, reflecting the national contexts of work and employment in which the actors are embedded, at the base of GVCs. To conceptualize vertical relations, I turn to the value chain governance theory proposed by Gereffi et al. (2005), who distinguish five governance types: market-based, modular, relational, captive, and hierarchical. These five types in turn can be defined according to three determinant variables: the complexity of transactions to be undertaken between buyers and suppliers, the ability to codify the transactions, and the capabilities of the supplier base. Furthermore, Gereffi et al. distinguish the degrees of explicit coordination and power asymmetry that exist in relationships of buyers and suppliers, such that market-based transactions feature the least explicit coordination and the lowest degree of power asymmetry, whereas hierarchical value chains exhibit the highest degrees. I add *workers* to these models, with reference to the three perspectives we have outlined, to acknowledge that each actor has a unique view on the prospects of identifying joint buyer, supplier, and worker interests in CSR. Finally, I expand the existing model by adding a consideration of how horizontal relations (national contexts of work and employment) influence the prospects of finding a sweet spot. I propose the analytical model of this optimum point for CSR in Table 1.1.

Market-Based Relations

With this model, I identify circumstances in which I anticipate convergence or divergence in buyer, supplier, and worker perspectives on the optimum point in CSR. In terms of vertical relations, if the interaction between buyers and suppliers is characterized by *market-based relations*, buyers likely cannot identify a point where they have joint interests with suppliers in CSR. The short-term

Table 1.1   A model of the sweet spot in CSR

	Market-Based Transactions	Relational Governance	Captive Governance	Hierarchy
Buyer perspective	No optimum point	Optimum-point (cooperative approach)	Optimum-point (compliance approach)	Optimum point
		National Contexts of Work and Employment		
Supplier perspective	No optimum point	No optimum point for SMEs	Optimum point for large suppliers	Optimum point for large suppliers
Worker perspective	No optimum point	No optimum point	Optimum point	Optimum point

Note: Here I discuss relational chains, not modular chains, reflecting my interest in the points at which we might find overlapping interests among buyers, suppliers, and workers by moving away from market-based conditions towards more explicit coordination in GVCs. In both modular and relational chains, suppliers tend to be highly capable and able to meet customer specifications. However, in modular value chains, due to their codification, information can be exchanged easily, which requires less explicit coordination, and the switching costs for buyers are lower, so buyer–supplier interactions resemble market-based settings. In relational chains, this relationship instead relies to a greater extent on mutual trust and dependence, so they require more explicit forms of coordination in the GVC.
Source: Adapted from Lund-Thomsen and Lindgreen (2018).

nature of these buyer–supplier interactions means that using either compliance or cooperative approaches would make little sense for buyers. Similarly, from the supplier perspective, there are few possibilities for identifying common interests with buyers in CSR, because these types of interactions are dominated by powerful price competition. For workers employed in supplier factories, the short-term nature of the work tasks required by market-based relations grants them few prospects for identifying an optimum point. Even if the national context is characterized by relatively strict labor laws and enforcement, the temporary nature of the commercial transactions between buyers and suppliers means that labor agency becomes highly constrained, providing little space for workers to align their interests with those of buyers or suppliers in CSR.

Relational Governance

For the case of relational governance between international buyers and first-tier suppliers in the analytical model, a different picture emerges. However, the main conclusion remains the same. That is, I still anticipate a likely divergence in the interests of buyers, suppliers, and workers in CSR. In detail, SME buyers with relatively few suppliers in the Global South often undertake relational governance, because in theory, they can develop longer-term trade relationships with SME suppliers, establish trust, and achieve mutual dependence. Such a scenario suggests that SME buyers would identify a potential sweet spot, through their use of a cooperative approach. In practice though, SME suppliers still face great difficulties in this effort, because even under relational governance, they are unlikely to operate according to the compliance-based norms and pressures that larger, more visible brands demand from suppliers. The prices paid may not be higher, even if these factories engage in longer-term transactions with their SME buyers. Production will still be seasonal, requiring the SMEs to hire and fire employees during the year without providing social security benefits to workers.

In horizontal relationships, the national contexts of work and employment seem more likely to influence suppliers' identification of an optimum point in CSR when the ties reflect relational governance rather than market-based relationships. For example, in Brazil, the presence of labor inspectorates and extensive public–private cooperation around the implementation of labor standards may reward SME suppliers for aligning their interests with their workers' and buyers'. However, in India, where the central government has linked economic development to a social downgrading strategy (i.e., not investing in worker protection; Knorringa and Nadvi, 2016), the national context of work and employment might prevent SME suppliers from aligning their interests with those of their workers (Khara and Lund-Thomsen, 2012). In relational governance settings, SME buyers may be able to identify an optimum point through a cooperative approach, but the national context of work and employment still might (not) provide incentives for SME suppliers to do so. The mutual dependence between SME buyers and SME suppliers that arises in relational governance contexts implies that horizontal relations should be more influential than vertical relations in terms of determining the prospects for identifying a sweet spot in CSR.

Captive Governance

In captive governance relations, I perceive greater prospects for establishing this optimum at which the interests of buyers, suppliers, and workers align. In captive chains, buyers from the Global North tend to work with many geographically dispersed suppliers, so buyers might prefer a compliance-based approach, to minimize risks to their reputation (i.e., avoid allegations or links to child or forced labor) across diverse national institutional contexts. From the perspective of large suppliers, codes of conduct and sustainability certifications may become part of their overall marketing strategies to appeal to international customers in the Global North. Similarly, for workers subject to captive forms of governance in the relations between international buyers and first-tier suppliers, stronger possibilities might arise for identifying an optimum point. Even if horizontal relations limit the scope for labor agency (i.e., by denying workers the right to collective bargaining, as in China as a case in point), vertical relations may overcome these restrictions to some extent, because large buyers tend to operate according to codes of conduct that go beyond the minimum requirements stipulated by national labor laws. That is, even in contexts that prohibit collective bargaining, buyers' power may be sufficient to enable collective forms of labor agency, such as in the form of wildcat strikes. At least in theory, such agency may help workers identify their sweet spot in CSR.

Hierarchy

Finally, for hierarchical governance relations, I anticipate the best prospects. The buyer retains ownership of the supplier, so it makes sense to adopt a cooperation-based approach, support capacity building, provide price incentives, and engage in joint production planning. Similarly, with their full integration into the parent (buyer) company, supplier factories likely can identify better prospects for aligned interests. Because the buyer retains ownership of the supplier, legal responsibility for the supplier's social performance falls back on the buyer; it is in the interest of both buyers and suppliers to take a cooperative approach to social upgrading that ensures the suppliers are responsive to headquarters' policies for responsible sourcing (vertical relations) and to national labor laws and enforcement agency requirements (horizontal relations). Hierarchical governance relationships also create greater chances for workers to identify their joint interests with buyers and suppliers. Because workers can directly negotiate the conditions of their work with their real employer (i.e., the buyer), rather than an intermediary supplier, they have substantially more space for effectively engaging in collective labor agency. Here again, vertical relations likely dominate horizontal relations in terms of enabling the identification of joint buyer, supplier, and worker interests in CSR, such that the positive or negative impacts of horizontal relations likely have less influence in hierarchical governance settings than is the case for relational governance.

Unsurprisingly, not all combinations make it possible to align the interests of buyers, suppliers, and workers in CSR. Instead, the prospects for identifying these joint interests improve significantly when we shift from market-based transactions towards hierarchical governance, as a function of the influence of vertical relations, though horizontal relations always mediate these prospects, in positive or negative directions. Whereas horizontal relations tend to be more important than vertical relations for influencing the alignment prospects under market-based and relational governance forms, vertical relations generally become more influential than horizontal relations under the captive and hierarchical forms.

LIMITATIONS OF THE ANALYTICAL FRAMEWORK

This theoretical model is well suited to analyze the interactions of international buyers and their first-tier suppliers in labor-intensive, export industries (e.g., garments, footwear, leather manufacturing), but it also has some limitations. First, it is not directly applicable to agricultural production networks. In agricultural networks, farmers rarely have any direct interaction with lead firms. Instead, the commodity (e.g., cotton) moves through several production tiers (ginning, trading, spinning, fabric mills, and sewing/stitching factories), before it winds up as part of the final product (e.g., a t-shirt) sold by international buyers (Alexander, 2016). In this sense, the model's applicability is limited to interactions of international buyers, their first-tier suppliers, and the workers who labor for the first-tier suppliers.

Second, it is possible to critique the underlying notion of a "sweet spot in CSR." This optimum point could appear unrealistic or even a misleading idea, in that it ignores the underlying, unequal battles between capital and labor in the highly dynamic, neo liberal, capitalist global economy. This challenge is particularly acute considering the criticisms of CSR for being Eurocentric, imposing a kind of North–South dichotomy on local producers and workers in developing countries (Khan and Lund-Thomsen, 2011; Ruwanpura, 2016). Admittedly, the theoretical model is somewhat static, whereas GVCs tend to be highly dynamic. The optimal points we identify thus may change constantly. In this light, the prospects for ensuring long-term trade relations, as envisaged in the cooperation paradigm, and the sweet spots within such trading relationships are likely limited.

Despite these limitations, three main policy implications flow from this analysis. First, for *multi-stakeholder initiatives* such as the UK-ETI and *buyers* in the Global North, there is no single blueprint for identifying a point at which buyers, suppliers, and workers all benefit in CSR. They must grant careful consideration to the changing nature of their GVC linkages (from market-based to hierarchical), the institutional context in which their GVCs function, and the different perspectives that buyers, suppliers, and workers likely adopt towards the optimum point in CSR, in that particular context. Before initiating any new interventions, a map of how these factors interact in given contexts would be useful, to maximize the prospects for identifying the common interests. Such mapping efforts already apply to assess human rights risks in particular countries; I suggest a similar method, with a view to establishing the prospects for identifying shifting sweet spots in particular industry and country contexts.

Noting the highly dynamic nature of GVCs, we suggest that such maps should be updated every six to twelve months.

Second, for *suppliers* in the Global South, this book highlights that their size and end markets matter in terms of whether they can identify joint interests in CSR. For large-scale suppliers that work with retailers and brands in the Global North, the prospects for aligning their interests with those of their buyers and suppliers are greater than they might be for SMEs. At the risk of oversimplifying the influence of GVC governance relationships, I argue that large-scale suppliers engaged in captive and hierarchical forms of governance with their buyers can meaningfully seek to identify their own sweet spot in CSR.

Third, for *workers*, the prospects for identifying joint interests are very complex; they depend, among other things, on factors such as the gender, age, livelihood strategies, reproductive concerns, and broader social networks of these workers. Regarding the influence of governance relationships, the prospects for labor agency tend to increase as we move from market-based relationships towards hierarchical governance. In other words, workers are more likely to identify joint interests with buyers and suppliers in captive and hierarchical governance conditions than in market-based or relational governance settings. However, with this prediction, I refer specifically to their prospects for collective labor agency.

This analytical model could be applied by both academics and policymakers to conduct further empirical research to identify optimum points in CSR in a variety of industry and country contexts. I hope that this analytical framework also provides foundations for a wider toolkit for practitioners, including retailers, suppliers, and trade unions, that seek a better understanding of the GVCs of which they are part, the labor rights risks contained therein, and the possibilities for workers to exercise labor agency within these networks.

OVERVIEW OF THE BOOK

In Chapter 2, I explore whether COVID-19 has led to a rethink of the two dominant ways of conceptualizing corporate social responsibility (CSR) in (GVCs): the compliance and cooperation paradigms. Hence, I examine whether any changes have taken place in the drivers, main features, theoretical underpinnings, and limitations of these two approaches to CSR in GVCs in the light of COVID-19. I contend that COVID-19 has been associated with an expanded version of the compliance paradigm. However, COVID-19 has not directly challenged the cooperation approach as a conceptual model. Instead the partial failure of buyers to act responsibly in relation to their purchasing practices and restrictions on international travel have highlighted the limitations of this approach in the age of COVID-19. The conclusion highlights the main findings, research, and policy implications of this analysis.

In Chapter 3, I develop a supplier-centered approach to corporate social responsibility (CSR) in (GVCs) by answering the research question: why are suppliers in the Global South that are integrated into GVCs often highly skeptical of CSR? As CSR constitutes a vague and contested term, I undertake a short review of some of the most dominant CSR conceptions that have emerged in the last 20 years. I argue that these CSR definitions are often framed and promoted by key actors in the Global North, the home of many lead firms, in ways that overlook the unique challenges and broader circumstances faced by suppliers and countries in the Global South. I conclude by combining the key considerations of local suppliers in a more consolidated supplier perspective on CSR in GVCs.

In Chapter 4, I move onto further unpacking a supplier-centered approach to CSR in GVCs by asking how industrial cluster dynamics and approaches to CSR can contribute to the social upgrading of women workers that participate in GVCs. I start from an overview of the gendered nature of GVCs, pointing out that the cluster literature has not yet sufficiently explored the gendered nature of social upgrading. I further unpack this argument by arguing that the insertion of local clusters into GVCs builds, in the case of gender, on a re-articulation of pre-existing gender inequalities in cluster settings in ways that benefit the dynamic functioning of GVCs. In this way, I suggest that a "devil's deal" may exist for social upgrading of women workers in industrial clusters. In fact, although local producer insertion in GVCs might facilitate local economic growth processes in industrial clusters, this could also simultaneously result in social downgrading of women workers in the same local regions. I conclude the chapter by arguing that supplier-driven collective CSR initiatives in local clusters in the Global South are unlikely to reverse this trend.

In Chapter 5, I examine the circumstances under which CSR initiatives facilitate and/or constrain labor agency in GVCs. Using a case of Nike's sourcing and CSR policies in the football manufacturing industry of Sialkot, Pakistan, I explore the extent to which the measures advocated in the cooperation-based paradigm on CSR in GVCs enabled and/or undermined labor agency in garment factories in Bangladesh during the early phases of COVID-19. I argue that while such CSR policies can create enhanced space for labor agency, that potential agency is also undermined by (i) wider economic forces within the global economy and (ii) relationships with local/national actors and regulatory frameworks. Understanding the intersection of these dimensions becomes vital to interpreting the potential and limitations for labor agency in GVCs.

Finally, the conclusion presents the main line of argument of the book and explores new research and policy options for moving beyond the current state of affairs in debates and practice on CSR in GVCs.

NOTES

1. Lund-Thomsen and Lindgreen (2014) refer to these two forms as compliance-based and cooperation-based approaches (see their Table 2).
2. Giant contractors also take on significant coordination functions in GVCs. Azmeh and Nadvi (2014) consider these giant contractors to be both strategic and pivotal, in that they perform critical functions, such as the design, manufacturing, and distribution of goods and services. Traditional lead firms also grant some network governance functions to these giants, so they orchestrate the flows of goods, components, capital, labor, and information throughout the network. They even might transform the network by rapidly switching production and sourcing arrangements from one country to another (Merk, 2014).
3. To respond to these challenges, some SMEs adopt cluster-based social upgrading initiatives (Giuliani, 2016). Clusters contain many firms, operating in the same or related industries, located together within a defined geographical space. In theory, this co-location enables cluster-based SMEs to adopt joint approaches to dealing with issues such as child labor (Lund-Thomsen et al., 2016). With the help of industry associations, they can pool their shared knowledge and financial resources, such that cluster-based SMEs should be able to facilitate the dissemination of social upgrading practices and improve compliance levels, more so than if they were to engage in social upgrading practices on their own (Puppim de Oliveira and Jabbour, 2017). Local, cluster-based adoption of corporate social responsibility practices by SMEs at the base of GVCs also might produce more locally relevant solutions to pressing labor issues, which may be preferable to the one-size-fits-all approaches of conventional compliance-based efforts (Lund-Thomsen and Nadvi, 2010b).

2.   Buyer perspectives

INTRODUCTION

In this chapter, I argue that the dramatic events of the first six months of 2020 provide us with an opportune moment to reflect on whether these recent developments have any direct implications for the dominant ways in which we conceptualize corporate social responsibility (CSR) in GVCs from the perspective of global buyers: the compliance and cooperation paradigms (see also, Lund-Thomsen and Lindgreen, 2014; Lund-Thomsen and Lindgreen, 2020). Hence, I revisit these two approaches to conceptualizing CSR in GVCs, critically (re)examining their drivers, main features, theoretical underpinnings, and limitations in the light of recent events that took place in the first eight months of COVID-19. I argue that the compliance paradigm can usefully be expanded to conceptual terms, whereas the cooperation paradigm in its traditional conception is still useful as an analytical approach to unpacking CSR in GVCs (Lund-Thomsen and Ramirez, 2020).

Following exposes of poor working conditions and child labor in the sub-contracted value chains of brands such as Nike and Levi Strauss in the 1990s, the so-called compliance-based paradigm to CSR in GVCs emerged (Gold et al., 2015). The main idea was that multinational retailers and brands should develop ethical guidelines for the social and environmental behavior of their suppliers, monitor the implementation of these guidelines through first-party, second-party, and third-party audits, and provide non-complying suppliers with a chance to rectify instances of non-compliance within a reasonable time period – for instance, six months (Lund-Thomsen and Lindgreen, 2014). If suppliers still did not comply with the buyers' ethical codes of conduct after this period, buyers were to punish non-complying factories by excluding them from their value chains (Locke, 2013).

By contrast, the cooperation-based paradigm highlighted the need for ensuring long-term cooperation between buyers and suppliers as a way of improving the latter's CSR performance (Locke et al., 2009). This involved buyers' rethinking their purchasing practices by incentivizing suppliers to improve work conditions by providing them with slightly higher unit prices for products (Amengual et al., 2020). Moreover, emphasis was placed on enabling suppliers to comply with buyers' codes of conduct by providing training to supplier management and workers in the stipulations of national labor laws, buyers' codes of conduct, and issues such as lean manufacturing (Distelhorst et al., 2016). Monitoring of working conditions should not be done through one-to three-day audits, but instead be undertaken 365 days a year through brand collaboration with local NGOs and trade unions (IDH, 2009). Finally, brand participation in multi-stakeholder initiatives was encouraged in the cooperation paradigm as brands working together with NGOs, suppliers, and other value chain actors was likely to have greater positive impacts on workers' conditions in GVCs (Riisgaard et al., 2020).

THE COMPLIANCE PARADIGM

Drivers

It still seems a sensible assumption that advocacy campaigns of NGOs and trade unions as well as media stories that expose poor working conditions and labor rights violations at the base of GVCs are a key driver of CSR in GVCs. For instance, on July 30, 2020, Danwatch – a Copenhagen-based advocacy organization – reported that it had found child labor in four out of six Fairtrade-certified cocoa farms during a "behind-the-scenes" investigation in the Ivory Coast in West Africa (Danwatch, 2020). Civil society campaigns also continue to apply pressure on global brands and retailers to change their sourcing practices – for instance, a coalition of 192 civil society organizations called upon apparel and textile brands to stop sourcing from the Uyghur region of China in which parts of the local population, Uyghurs, were compelled to engage in forced labor in prison-like camps and other workplaces (Coalition, 2020).

However, with the advent of COVID-19, it no longer seems realistic to assume that it is only NGOs, trade unions, and media outlets that expose unethical sourcing practices and poor labor conditions at supplier factories, as was a key assumption in the compliance paradigm. For instance, in early 2020, as buyers in the Global North began to cancel or delay orders to their suppliers and failed to pay for existing orders, it became increasingly obvious that millions of workers would suffer not only the short-term losses of jobs but also that their own and wider family's well-being might be at risk – especially in cases where workers and their families had no alternative sources of income (Anner, 2020). At the time, a coalition of Western academics, NGOs and advocacy organizations along with suppliers from the Global South (Bangladesh in particular) initiated a joint campaign that would seek to ensure that retailers and brands would "pay up" whatever they owed in terms of financial resources to their supplier factories in the Global South (Leitheiser et al., 2020). This was institutionalized through a so-called COVID-19 tracker – established by the United States-based labor advocacy organization – the Workers' Rights Consortium – that highlighted which garment and textile brands had made a commitment to pay in full for orders completed and in production and which brands were yet to do so (if at all) (Workers' Rights Consortium, 2020). It is interesting to note that such a COVID-tracker could not have been established without active support from some factories, particularly in Bangladesh that appear to have provided the necessary information, making it possible to establish and maintain the list. Hence, in terms of drivers behind the compliance paradigm, I argue that we need to expand our conception of the actors that drive a compliance-based paradigm from not only including NGOs, trade unions, and media outlets to also include supplier factories in the Global South.

Clearly, COVID-19 does not mark the first time that brands' purchasing practices have been under critical scrutiny (Barrientos and Smith, 2007). In fact, the purchasing practices of global brands have long been recognized as being a driver behind labor rights violations at supplier factories in the Global South (Amengual et al., 2020). These include late orders compelling workers to do overtime, buyers' price squeeze driving down wages of workers at supplier factories, and unstable demand resulting in the frequent firing and rehiring of workers that could not be hired on permanent contracts due to the volatility of global demand (Khan et al., 2020). An initiative such as Better Buying has thus allowed suppliers to anonymously rate the purchasing practices of their buyers and inform brands and retailers about which practices can be improved (Better Buying, 2020).

Hence, I suggest that we need to modify our understanding of the term "compliance." It should not encompass supplier compliance with buyer codes of conduct, but also relate to global brands complying with what may be considered fair and ethical purchasing practices in their GVCs.

Main Features

I now turn to a critical examination of whether we need to reconceptualize the main features of the compliance paradigm in the light of COVID-19. My first argument is that many of the key features of the compliance paradigm can still be maintained in this theoretical approach. Some of the events of 2020 are good illustrations of how "old" labor rights compliance challenges such as ensuring the occupational health and safety of workers have reappeared in new forms. For instance, avoiding industrial "accidents" in export-oriented factories has traditionally been a challenge, leading to a situation where workers were required to wear facemasks if they were handling dangerous chemicals (Barrientos and Smith, 2007). During COVID-19, export-oriented factories in the garments industry of Asia supplying global brands were suddenly required to introduce procedures and training regarding social distancing, the use of facemasks, and frequent washing of hands (Axfoundation, 2020). Hence, there have particularly been concerns around migrant workers living in overcrowded hostels at factory sites where it has not been possible for them to observe social distancing in ways that are usually recommended by health specialists (Channel 4, 2020).

Another example of how it is still relevant to maintain existing conceptions of CSR compliance challenges in GVCs is overtime. For instance, given the huge initial imbalances between world demand and supply of hand sanitizers and facemasks, factories in the healthcare sector were suddenly compelled to expand world production in a very short time (Gereffi, 2020). In terms of implications for labor rights compliance, a UK Channel 4 news investigation found in June 2020 that the world's largest manufacturer of protective gloves – Top Glove – had workers undertake 12-hour long work shifts, that some workers managed to clock up 111 hours of overtime in a month in breach of Malaysian labor laws, and that the workers feared catching COVID-19 due to poor social distancing arrangements at the factory and worker hostel sites (Channel 4, 2020).

I would furthermore suggest that our existing conception of CSR compliance challenges can be maintained if we look at the example of the social insurance of workers. Ensuring that workers have social insurance – that is, health insurance, unemployment insurance, and old age retirement benefits – turned out to be particularly challenging during COVID-19. With a sudden decline in demand in particular product types in early 2020, garments and textile, factories in supplier countries such as India, Pakistan, and Bangladesh were forced to dismiss thousands if not millions of workers within a very short time span (Anner, 2020). Typically, this was associated with non-compliance with buyer codes of conduct in relation to issues such as proper notice before worker dismissal, payment of proper compensation, and compensation for hospital bills (and in some cases worker deaths) as a result of COVID-19 (ETI, 2020).

My second argument is, that we need to expand our conceptualization of CSR monitoring in the compliance paradigm to include (a) desk-based and (b) virtual monitoring in addition to on-site monitoring of work conditions. For instance, with the advent of COVID-19, "on-site" first- and third-party monitoring of labor conditions in garment factories were sometimes difficult to undertake due to lock-downs in many countries in Asia and reduced possibilities for international (and sometimes national) travel (Rankin, 2020). Here I would argue that desk-based research can be seen as an important complement to on-site monitoring in the compliance-based paradigm. For instance, desk-based research labor rights monitoring is often conducted as part of human rights due diligence in GVCs. Human rights due diligence can help brands in reducing the risk of buyers that they are involved in trading relationships that involve the use of, for example, child labor or forced labor (European Coalition for Corporate Justice, 2020). Hence, such assessments do not only involve "on-site" social auditing but also involve desk-based research that aims at detecting evidence from multiple sources – previous reports, expert interviews via phone/SKYPE/other social media, reviews of news media and other sources that could indicate the potential risk of companies becoming involved in human rights violations in their value chains as well as developing procedures for ensuring that there are grievance mechanisms in place for workers.

Moreover, I contend that virtual monitoring must be understood as an important part of the compliance-based paradigm. For instance, during COVID-19, virtual monitoring has, in some instances, been used as a supplement to traditional on-site, audit-based monitoring (Rina, 2020). For instance, UK-based labor rights consultancy, Impactt Limited (2011) worked with brand suppliers and workers in remotely monitoring work conditions at factory sites when physical visits were made difficult due to COVID-19 travel restrictions. In practice, Impactt obtained a list of employees and phone numbers from brand supplier factories, and undertook "remote" worker interviews via phone, WhatsApp, or other online communication tools at a time and location chosen by the workers themselves. While this method did not permit for first-hand impressions of workers conditions in the same way as physical visits would have done, it did make it possible to gather some rudimentary information about workers' conditions (Pyle, 2020).

My third argument is that we must reconceptualize central features of the compliance paradigm: that is, that suppliers may receive increased orders due to compliance with labor codes of conduct and be excluded by brands from GVC participation due to non-compliance with these corporate codes of conduct. I still support this theoretical contention, but I also suggest that we need to include the option that supplier factories may exclude particular brands from their GVCs due to non-compliance with ethical purchasing practices.

As mentioned above, in March/April 2020, when many global brands and retailers were compelled to temporarily close their physical retail outlets in Europe and North America, the attention of some (but not all!) retailers and brands in the garment industry turned to securing their survival by engaging in cost-cutting exercises (for instance, sometimes laying off some of their CSR/sustainability staff), canceling or delaying orders, or not paying for orders already completed before these products were sold in Europe or North America (Leitheiser et al., 2020). However, these purchasing practices also led to threats from organizations such as the Bangladesh Garments Manufacturers and Exporters Association (BGMEA) to boycott particular brands. For instance, BGMEA has considered issuing a list of brands and retailers that were banned from sourcing from Bangladesh as long as they had not paid up on the dues that they owed Bangladeshi manufacturers (Cline, 2020). Excluding "unethical" brands and retailers from supplier value chains would – in theory – lead to a reversal of the compliance model. In other words, in addition to non-compliant factories being excluded from brands' or retailers' value chains, I suggest that CSR non-compliant brands and retailers may – at least in theory – be excluded from the value chains of suppliers in the Global South.

Theoretical Underpinnings

The compliance-based paradigm has traditionally been theoretically under-pinned by the GVC approach (Lund-Thomsen and Lindgreen, 2014). The GVC approach has emphasized that role of multinational companies, or so-called lead firms, in organizing their vast networks of suppliers across the globe (Ponte, 2019). In the GVC approach, these lead firms govern these chains – in other words, they decided which kinds of products are to be produced where, when, in which quantity, at what price, and under what social and environmen-tal conditions by their supplier across the world (Gereffi, 2019). In the GVC approach, local suppliers are then seen as having different opportunities for improving their competitive position in these chains by improving the quality of their products ("product upgrading"), the efficiency of their production processes ("process upgrading"), moving into higher value-added functions of the chain such as branding and marketing ("chain upgrading"), and using skills learned from competing in one industry to gain competitive advantage in another industry ("interchain upgrading") (Ponte et al., 2019).

In my view, GVC analysis remains useful as a theoretical foundation for the compliance-based paradigm in the age of COVID-19. However, we have to apply theoretical concepts such as lead firm governance and supplier upgrad-ing to not only examine CSR in value chains on a *global scale*. According to the WTO, world trade reached its peak at the time of the global financial crisis in 2007/2008 and has since been on the decline. Hence, already prior to COVID-19, there were debates about the possible emergence of regional value chains and potentially even the reshoring of some aspects of labor-intensive manufacturing from Global South to Global North locations (Gereffi, 2020). In other words, the questions of *where to produce* and *when to produce* were already parts of international debates on sustainable sourcing prior to COVID-19, particularly in relation to reducing lead times and ensuring alter-native sources of supply (Butollo, 2020). The pre-occupation with ensuring alternative sources of supply had also been on the table given the ongoing trade war between China and the United States, leading many retailers and brands to encourage their suppliers to move production out of China to other manufactur-ing locations in Asia and elsewhere. The impact of COVID-19 – with massive worldwide disruptions of GVCs – has reinforced debates about whether global retailers and brands would need to restructure their value chains so that they procured goods and services mainly through *regional* or *domestic* value chains instead of *GVCs*, which have been so dominant throughout the last 30 years (Gereffi, 2020). Hence, I would suggest that we should increasingly focus on seeing the compliance-based paradigm as not only applicable to GVC analysis but also relevant for the analysis of CSR in regional and domestic value chains.

An Expanded Compliance Paradigm and Its Limitations

In short, I believe that we need to expand our current understanding of the compliance paradigm to CSR in GVCs. In its basic version, this paradigm still relates to: (a) corporate codes of conduct being used by lead firms to regulate work conditions at supplier factories; (b) first-, second-, and third-party monitoring of compliance taking place at these suppliers; (c) suppliers being given time to implement corrective plans in case of non-compliance with buyer codes of conduct; and (d) buyers excluding suppliers from their value chains if they continuously fail to come into compliance with the buyer's code of conduct. In the light of COVID-19, I argue that our understanding of compliance monitoring needs to be expanded. Hence, in my reconceptualization, the model now envisages compliance monitoring as not only taking place through on-site auditing but it also through virtual or distance monitoring (see also Pyle, 2020).

Moreover, in the light of COVID-19, I suggest that the compliance paradigm should be modified so that compliance with corporate codes of conduct – at least in theory – is not only expected from suppliers but also from buyers (Lund-Thomsen, 2020). Hence, in the expanded version, the compliance paradigm includes corporate codes of conduct being developed for the purchasing practices of buyers, including the possibility that suppliers exclude buyers from their value chains in case buyers continuously fail to comply with these codes. In the expanded compliance paradigm, codes of conduct for buyer purchasing practices then stipulate that: (a) brands should not cancel already confirmed orders, (b) brands should not delay payments for existing orders, and (c) brands should not fail to pay suppliers altogether for orders already placed.

Limitations of An Expanded Compliance Paradigm

If we consider the limitations of such an expanded compliance-based paradigm, several challenges emerge. First, I would argue that brands and retailers are unlikely to universally sign up for codes of conduct that regulate their purchasing practices, as this is likely to directly constrain their possibilities for procuring products and services at the lowest possible price at the time and place of their own preference (Lund-Thomsen, 2020). Second, the idea that suppliers exclude buyers from their value chains due to non-compliance with codes of conduct on buyer practices may still be somewhat theoretical. Often suppliers rely on a few customers, and their business may be severely hampered if they lose existing orders, even if they only receive "razor thin" margins from these buyers. Third, I would argue that suppliers may also be unlikely to "rock-the-boat" even if they may be legally entitled to compensation under their existing contracts with buyers. Hence, suppliers are less likely to take buyers to court in Europe and the United States, as this requires capital, time and human resource investments that many suppliers may not have (Ward, 2003). Moreover, launching legal challenges against your buyers for violating existing contracts may put suppliers at risk in terms of other buyers shying away from doing business with these local producers. Hence, many suppliers are unlikely on an individual basis to sue their buyers for non-compliance with existing order contracts.

Third, with it comes compliance monitoring with corporate codes of conduct at the level of suppliers, it is not only audits but also the new compliance monitoring approaches that are associated with particular challenges (Lund-Thomsen, 2020). Just as creating false paper trails regarding workers' salaries, work hours and age; coaching workers; and bribing auditors have long been recognized as weaknesses of using traditional on-site factory audits, using the expanded data collection methods promoted by human rights and environmental due diligence approaches may also face similar challenges in gathering the required data (Egels-Zandén, 2007; Lebaron and Lister, 2015).

A particular risk associated with buyers using human rights and environmental due diligence approaches to ensure supplier compliance appears to be that they mainly encourage brands and retailers to "clean" their value chains of forced labor, child labor, and other labor rights violations rather than pro-actively seeking to develop solutions that address these complex issues (Lund-Thomsen, 2020). Hence, using human rights and environmental due diligence approaches may be used by buyers as a cover to evade rather than accept responsibility for actively using their financial resources, know-how and management skills to support both what has become known as "social upgrading" in the GVC literature – that is, improving the conditions, rights, and entitlements of workers in these chains (Lund-Thomsen and Ramirez, 2020).

Similarly, while remote monitoring of work conditions (in addition to site auditing of work conditions at factory sites) may provide some rudimentary insights into work conditions and possibly labor rights violations in the value chain (Pyle, 2020), they will likely always remain a second-best solution when compared to conducting on-site inspections of factories. At least, the challenges of workers being coached, possibly threatened if they reveal particular violations, and bribery of auditors do not simply go away, because monitoring is now conducted at a distance. With this in mind, I turn now to a critical re-examination of whether we need to reconceptualize the drivers, main features, conceptual underpinnings, and limitations of the cooperation paradigm in the light of the events experienced in early 2020.

COOPERATION PARADIGM

Drivers

It was a wide coalition of actors that first promoted the adoption of the cooperation paradigm in the early 2000s. Amongst CSR staff in certain brands, there was an increasing frustration with the expensive use of audits that often provided limited insights into the real nature of work conditions in supplier factories at the base of GVCs (Lund-Thomsen and Lindgreen, 2014). Some CSR consultants also felt that it was necessary to use alternatives to traditional auditing in order to ensure not only better insights into "the real picture" regarding work conditions in export-oriented factories, but also to improve the chances of improving work conditions at the base of GVCs in the Global South (IDH, 2009). Moreover, some development NGOs and academics highlighted the shortcomings of the compliance paradigm in various policy and academic publications as well as more public presentations that generated industry-wide attention to the need for alternatives to traditional auditing methods (Oka et al., 2020a).

Interestingly, anecdotal evidence suggests that the coalition of actors that have advocated for the adoption of a more cooperation-based approach to CSR in GVCs may have widened in the wake of COVID-19. In fact, the same coalition of actors that highlighted the unethical purchasing practices of some global brands and retailers after the eruption of COVID-19 in early 2020 may also be viewed as the actors that would (at least implicitly) advocate some of the main features of the cooperation-based paradigm. However, an interesting aspect to the campaign was that a new actor – Global South-based suppliers – joined the campaign by helping labor rights advocates in identifying those brands that had honored existing contracts and payment schedules and those that had not (Lund-Thomsen, 2020). This change in the types of actors and coalitions who pushed for improvements in the rights and conditions of workers at the base of GVCs in the Global South illustrates the dynamic nature of not only GVC organization but also the wider networks of actors that seek to actively influence the functioning and power dynamics present in these chains.

Main Features

In theoretical terms, a key feature of the cooperation paradigm is a focus on revising purchasing practices of global brands and retailers in ways that would enable their suppliers to comply with their corporate codes of conduct (Lund-Thomsen and Lindgreen, 2014). However, the events of early 2020 also demonstrated that the expectations of the cooperative paradigm do not correspond to the actual behavior of many brands (if brands and retailers ever did!). In fact, rather than strengthening long-term trade relations with their suppliers in 2020, some brands and retailers resorted to short-term measures such as cutting ties or not honoring contracts made with their suppliers, causing financial hardship – both for the suppliers and the millions of workers that depended upon more stable trade relationships between global buyers and their suppliers in the Global South (Leitheiser et al., 2020). Moreover, instead of paying a little extra for their products in order to help suppliers make the factory investments that would enable them to be more socially compliant, some Western brands and retailers sought to renegotiate prices in a downwards fashion in early 2020 (Anner, 2020).

However, the picture is not uniform. The expectations of the cooperation paradigm that brands are willing to revise (or at least reconsider) their purchasing practices appear to have been validated by some other brands. According to the COVID-19 tracker, some brands and retailers did confirm their willingness and commitment to honoring existing contracts and continue their long-term engagement with their suppliers (Workers' Rights Consortium, 2020). Hence, the events of early 2020 both confirm and challenge the expectations of the cooperation paradigm regarding buyers revising their purchasing practices and engaging in long-term trading relations with their suppliers. Hence, I would argue that we need to refine the cooperation paradigm so that the expectation is that only some brands are willing to engage in CSR in GVCs by revising their purchasing practices and engaging in long-term trade relations with their suppliers, whereas other, more 'footloose' brands should be expected to engage in 'social irresponsible behavior' by failing to honor existing contracts, continuously squeezing prices, and promoting a race-to-the-bottom by seeking to obtain the cheapest deal wherever possible.

The cooperation paradigm had previously also advocated that brands and retailers could facilitate social compliance at their supplier factories by providing training to factory management and workers that would ensure that they had greater knowledge and awareness of national labor laws and their buyers' code of conduct (Amengual et al., 2020). By providing this training, it was thought that supplier management would be in a better position to adapt factory operations to comply with relevant national labor laws and buyers' requirements (Locke, 2013). At the same time, it was considered that training workers in their rights would enable them to apply pressure on their employers to improve working conditions within local factory settings (Lund-Thomsen and Coe, 2015).

The events of early 2020 in the garments industry seem to confirm the expectation of the cooperative paradigm that (at least) some brands and retailers are willing to engage in the capacity building of their suppliers and workers at the base of their GVCs. Hence, some brands and multi-stakeholder initiatives retain a focus on training factory management and trade unions in social dialogue as a way of resolving industrial disputes in a mutually benefi-cial manner (Danish Ethical Trading Initiative, 2020). However, COVID-19 has also in its early phases led to a diversion of some of these training efforts to address more immediate concerns related to contagion, such as training factory management and workers in how to ensure social distancing and that workers carry out the hygiene necessary to avoid the spread of coronavirus (such as washing hands regularly), as well as reshaping the production floor in ways that allow for continued production of goods and services albeit at a reduced pace in some factories (Axfoundation, 2020). In this way, capacity-building activities appear to continuously evolve over time in response to changing needs of suppliers and workers. I suggest that the cooperative paradigm can usefully be modified to understand capacity building as not only a more static activity with focus on particular activities but also as a more dynamic activity that can be adapted to changing GVC circumstances.

Another central feature of the cooperation paradigm has been to avoid short-term social audits that led to a rather superficial assessment of work conditions within factories. Instead the cooperation paradigm advocated the year-round engagement of "local resources" such as NGOs and trade unions that could provide a more nuanced and long-term assessment of work condi-tions within particular factories (Lund-Thomsen and Lindgreen, 2014). This trend also involves conducting off-site interviews with workers that could provide more detailed accounts of the work conditions and work life within particular factories without workers having to be concerned about facing puni-tive actions from their employers in instances where they might criticize labor rights abuses within factories (Bartley and Egels-Zandén, 2015).

The eruption of COVID-19 in early 2020 seems to have confirmed this assumption of the cooperation paradigm: that is, that brands continuously use local resources to monitor work conditions at supplier factories. As argued above, organizations such as the UK-based consultancy Impactt have increasingly experimented with "monitoring at a distance." For instance, by conducting interviews with workers at a time or place at the convenience of workers through online applications such as WhatsApp or SKYPE against lists provided by factory management. Monitoring at a distance has emerged as a tool that could also be used through pre-existing networks – for instance,

NGOs having community organizers already present in areas where factory workers live – thus ensuring the immediate proximity to workers who could be interviewed in a more informal basis via phone even if meeting up physically was not always an option (Rankin, 2020).

The expectation of the cooperative paradigm that brands and retailers will engage in multi-stakeholder initiatives (MSIs) to join forces in order to boost their CSR in GVC work also seems to be confirmed by actual events during the first eight months of 2020 (Lund-Thomsen and Ramirez, 2020). However, the move away from on-site meetings of large multi-stakeholder audiences have also meant that a lot of the information and knowledge exchange so characteristic of the functioning of MSIs shifted to online formats in 2020 (such as Pyle, 2020). Typically, these involve the increasing use of webinars and online conferences that serve to heighten awareness of the current state of play in relation to labor rights issues and work conditions in GVCs that touch down in various contexts (Danish Ethical Trade Initiative, 2020). In this way, the initial experience with COVID-19 in the garments industry in early 2020 confirms the assumption of the cooperative paradigm that brand collaboration through MSIs is a critical factor in improving conditions of workers at the base of GVCs in the Global South.

Theoretical Underpinnings

Behind the cooperation paradigm has been a vision of the world economy being organized through global production networks rather than GVCs per se (Coe and Yeung, 2015a). Whereas the GVC literature has traditionally focused more narrowly on interfirm relationships between international buyers and suppliers, the global production networks approach has understood the organization of transnational industries as also involving a wider spectrum of actors such as NGOs, trade unions, government organizations, banks, other financial institutions, and other stakeholders that play a role in influencing and regulating the functioning of these GVCs (Lund-Thomsen, 2020). The global production networks approach has also emphasized the multi-scalar nature of production networks (ranging from the global to the national, regional, and local levels of analysis) and the evolutionary nature of global production networks – that is, such networks change significantly over time. A particular strength of the global production networks approach has also been its concern with the local institutional context in which global production networks were embedded (Coe and Yeung, 2019). In fact, such contexts in a diversity of countries across the world have been understood to influence the functioning of global production networks in ways that created divergent outcomes for regional economic and social development – including in the Global South (Bae et al., 2020).

In my view, the global production networks approach remains very valid as a theoretical underpinning of the cooperation approach to CSR in the age of COVID-19. Seeing transnational industries as organized through networks rather than chains may be helpful in explaining the influence of governmental regulators in trying to influence the providers of health equipment – for instance, by buying up international stocks of facemasks, or alternatively, instituting export bans on health equipment considered to be vital to national security (Gereffi, 2020). COVID-19 has also highlighted the need to engage in multi-scalar analysis in ways that illustrate the importance of not only looking at international developments in relation to the functioning of global production networks, but also looking at more regional, national, and/or local trajectories in the disruption and resumption of the functioning of these chains (Lund-Thomsen and Ramirez, 2020).

The same point can also be made in relation to various institutional contexts, both in the Global North and Global South that influence the functioning of global production networks. For instance, in early 2020, COVID-19 affected China in ways that led to an immediate disruption of exports from that country. Hence, COVID-19 first had a significant impact on supply. However, as we moved into March and April 2020 when COVID-19 took hold of markets in Europe and North America, country-wide lock-downs and the forced closing of retail outlets let to a dramatic reduction in global demand for products such as textiles and garments from manufacturers in China (Lund-Thomsen, 2020). Hence, the focus of the global production networks approach on local institutional contexts and the evolutionary nature of these networks seems very appropriate when analyzing CSR in such networks within the cooperation paradigm. This can also be witnessed in the context of India, for instance, where the national government decided to change existing labor laws in ways that may ease the cost of doing business for Indian companies after the eruption of COVID-19 in early 2020 but also appear to weaken the rights of workers that participate in global, national, and local value chains in the country (BBC News, 2020). Hence, an important theoretical implication from COVID-19 appears to be that context still matters in the analysis of the functioning of transnational industries. The impacts of COVID-19 on the organization and functioning of these industries need to be interpreted with due regard to the varied experiences of retailers, brands, suppliers, and workers across these different contexts.

Limitations

The dramatic events of early 2020 in the global garments industry do not – in my view – suggest that we fundamentally need to rethink the cooperation paradigm as a conceptual model. Instead the fundamental tenets of the cooperation paradigm should still be conceptualized as: (a) the revision of buyer purchasing practices, (b) capacity building of factory management and workers in buyer codes of conduct and local labor laws, (c) the use of local resources in year-round monitoring of labor conditions in local factories, and (d) the participation of brands and suppliers in multi-stakeholder initiatives as a road towards promoting CSR in GVCs.

Instead future studies of CSR in GVCs will likely determine whether clothing brands and retailers actually followed the prescriptions of the cooperation paradigm in their immediate response to COVID-19 in early 2020. A very cursory reading of public newspaper and media reporting of these events would appear to indicate that some brands and retailers markedly deviated in their behavior from the prescriptions of the cooperation paradigm. For these brands renegotiating prices with their suppliers in a downwards direction and not honoring existing contracts appear to have been an important part of their response to COVID-19 in early 2020 (see, for instance, Anner, 2020). However, it also appeared as if other brands committed to honoring their existing contracts and continued trading relations with many of their suppliers with a view to ensuring the longer-term resilience of their value chains (Leitheiser et al., 2020). In my view, this does not challenge the basic expectations of the cooperation paradigm – namely that both brands and suppliers can enhance their CSR in GVC performance by engaging in longer-term, more committed trading relations. However, in practice, the cooperation paradigm may have been more of an inspirational model – a kind of ideal that clothing brands and retailers could aspire towards, but which might not always be practically feasible to practice in a context of cut-throat, price-based competition with rapid changes in demand and supply (Lund-Thomsen and Lindgreen, 2014).

Moreover, I still believe that the cooperation paradigm's prediction that brands/retailers will support the training of local factory managers and workers in buyer codes of conduct/labor laws remains valid. During COVID-19, anecdotal evidence suggests that some brands have supported worker training in areas related to social distancing, the use of sanitizers, and facemasks (Axfoundation, 2020). Furthermore, it also appears that some brands and retailers have continued the use of local resources who can assist in the monitoring of labor conditions at supplier factories, now also as part of "distance monitoring" (Pyle, 2020). And finally, while detailed empirical studies are yet to be carried out on the functioning of MSIs in the garment industry during COVID-19, it would still appear that the cooperation paradigm's emphasis on the importance of brand involvement in these initiatives continues to hold true. At least, many MSIs continued to function in 2020, promoting the exchange of information and collaboration around CSR in GVCs, including on the important topic of how brand, supplier, and worker representatives could adjust their CSR in GVC strategies during the crisis.

CONCLUSION

In this chapter, I argued that it was important to revisit the two dominant approaches (the compliance and cooperation paradigms) to conceptualizing CSR in GVCs in the light of the dramatic events that took place in early 2020 in the global garment industry. Specifically, I posed the question: do we need to rethink the drivers, main features, theoretical underpinnings, and limitations of both paradigms in the light of the lights of recent events? I argued that we should adjust the compliance paradigm as a conceptual model by not only seeing "compliance" as related to suppliers abiding by buyers' corporate codes of conduct. Instead I argued that "compliance" must also be viewed as global buyers abiding by ethical purchasing and trading practices. Moreover, I suggested that CSR compliance monitoring must not only be seen as related to on-site factory audits. Compliance monitoring in GVCs also includes wider human rights due diligence approaches and the use of distance monitoring. Finally, I suggested that the compliance paradigm should be adjusted to recognize that value chain exclusion due to "non-compliance" with dominant CSR norms and values in GVCs can both involve factories and brands/retailers. In other words, we can – at least theoretically – imagine situations, in which suppliers "blacklist" brands and retailers from their value chains due to their non-compliance with ethical purchasing practices.

However, I also posited that the cooperation paradigm – as a conceptual model – does not need to be rethought or even adjusted in the light of recent events associated with COVID-19. On the contrary, the paradigm's emphasis on ensuring long-term trading partnerships between brands and suppliers and reconsidering purchasing practices seem increasingly relevant in order to mitigate the negative impacts of sudden changes in demand or supply on buyers, suppliers, and workers. In other words, from the perspective of the cooperation paradigm, COVID-19 has highlighted a situation in which brands, suppliers, and workers sometimes "swim or sink" together during the eruption of a worldwide crisis such as COVID-19.

However, one thing is the paradigm's prediction that long-term cooperation between brands and suppliers is likely to improve workers' conditions in GVCs. Another is the stark empirical reality that the behavior of some garment brands and retailers did not follow the path recommended by the cooperation paradigm during the early phases of 2020. Instead these actors appeared to be guided by short-term survival considerations: price-cutting, cancellation of orders, and failure to pay for already placed orders. These events seemed to confirm the limitations associated with the cooperation paradigm which had already been acknowledged prior to the outbreak of 2020 (see Lund-Thomsen and Lindgreen, 2014). Namely, that the cooperation paradigm may be an interesting conceptual model, but that the world of global commerce is often dominated by worldwide, cut-throat competition between suppliers in different countries in ways that undermine any realistic prospects for CSR in GVCs being guided by long-term benefits and a sweet spot where the interests of buyers, suppliers, and workers rarely intersect in mutually beneficial ways.

A point of critique of these two contrasting buyer perspectives on CSR in GVCs could be that they are not as different as they immediately seem. As the title of this chapter implies, they are indeed both buyer-driven, and mainly view retailers and brands as having the power to control and steer their vast networks of suppliers around the world. I would here of course agree that both approaches assume that retailers and brands are indeed such powerful actors in GVCs. However, I would still argue that it makes a difference to both suppliers and workers, if retailers and brands mainly adopt a compliance or a cooperation approach. For instance, in recent times, there has been widespread media coverage in Europe regarding the *potential* involvement of Uyghur migrant workers, laboring under slave-like conditions in Chinese factories that produced facemasks for European importers of medical devices and equipment. Here European importers can choose a more narrow, short-term compliance-oriented approach and quickly discontinue trading relations with these factories, in ways that can negatively affect the bottom-line of the Chinese exporters, potentially leading to lay-offs. Another route implies that the European importers invest in longer-term relations with their Chinese suppliers – which, in case the suppliers display active willingness to improve conditions – and engage in a cooperation approach that helps to upgrade both local management and workers, improving the conditions of the latter, or at least, ensuring that no Uyghur workers are employed against their will at the factories. In my understanding, it can have very direct consequences for suppliers and workers, whether brands and retailers mainly operate through a compliance or a cooperation lens on CSR in GVCs.

Another point of contention may be that brands and retailers in practice employ a combination of compliance and cooperation approaches – a kind of combined carrot and stick approach to CSR in GVCs. Hence, it could be argued that the compliance and cooperation approaches are oversimplified in their conceptualization of buyer approaches to CSR in GVCs. I would agree that brands and retailers typically employ a combination of both approaches in practice. However, I would still maintain that it makes sense to keep this rather stylistic representation of buyer-driven CSR, because there may be real tensions between compliance and cooperation approaches when brands and retailers, or multi-stakeholder initiatives for that matter, simultaneously employ them at the base of value chains in the Global South.

In a recent study, I was part of a research team that documented how a multi-stakeholder initiative, the Better Cotton Initiative, was both engaged in capacity building and compliance monitoring of farmers who were supposed to produce more sustainable forms of cotton in India and Pakistan (Lund-Thomsen et al., 2018). On the one hand, the Better Cotton Initiative (BCI) used intermediaries such as NGOs, private-sector suppliers, and philanthropic foundations to build the capacity of farmers to comply with the BCI's sustainable cotton standard. On the other hand, the same intermediaries, along with third-party auditors, were involved in monitoring whether the farmers complied with the standard. Hence, the mixture of cooperation and compliance approaches meant that the BCI sought to empower farmers, giving them the ability to produce cotton in a more productive and socially/environmentally sustainable way. Simultaneously, monitoring farmers implied that farmers had to gather a lot of data to demonstrate compliance with the standard, and that the BCI sought to exert "power over" these farmers by tightly monitoring their behavior. In practice, such contradictory ways of engaging with farmers sometimes made it difficult for the intermediaries that we studied to convince farmers of the benefits that they would derive from being licensed as BCI farmers (Lund-Thomsen et al., 2021).

Finally, one might also question whether all brands and retailers necessarily follow either or both of these approaches to CSR in GVCs. For instance, does it not matter whether these brands and retailers are located in particular home country environments? For instance, does it not matter whether Nike based in the United States or Adidas based in Germany work with either or both approaches? In a previous study, I documented that Nike appeared to have a more "zero-tolerance" approach towards child labor in its value chains (Lund-Thomsen, 2013). In other words, if child labor were found in one of its subcontracted value chains, Nike would – at the time the study was conducted – most likely terminate relations with that supplier (Lund-Thomsen and Coe, 2015). However, its main rival, German-based sports brand, Adidas, did not necessarily have the same approach towards dealing with the possible existence of child labor in its value chains. In fact, Adidas might be more willing to work with the suppliers to find remediation approaches at the time that we conducted the study, finding education alternatives for the child and/or alternative income generation opportunities for the child's family, so that the child was no longer working at the supplier, but without this meaning that Adidas necessarily terminated its contract with the supplier in question (see also, Lund-Thomsen and Nadvi, 2010b). Hence, as other authors have also demonstrated there may be significant differences between the CSR approaches adopted by companies that have different host countries (Matten and Moon, 2008; Jamali, 2010).

This is also a theme that I explore in the next chapter that explores supplier perceptions of CSR in GVCs.

3.   Supplier-centered perspectives

INTRODUCTION

Prior to COVID-19, some economic geographers and development studies scholars had already begun to focus on the role played by CSR in GVCs (Lund-Thomsen and Coe, 2015; Ruwanpura and Wrigley, 2011). Some of this work reported that suppliers struggled to navigate the competing demands of price pressures, shortened lead times, and social compliance demands from their buyers (Khan et al., 2020; Raj-Reichert, 2013; Ruwanpura and Wrigley, 2011). The journal *Global Networks* also dedicated a special issue to CSR in GVCs in 2015 (Bair and Palpacuer, 2015). The special issue contained papers devoted to a diversity of topics, such as corporate codes of conduct; NGOs and social movements in GVCs; global framework agreements; and global carbon chains, and firms' "social license to operate" in GVCs (Bartley and Egels-Zandén, 2015; Böhm et al., 2015; Fichter and McCallum, 2015; Mayes, 2015; Nickow, 2015). Moreover, a special issue of the *Journal of Business Ethics* on CSR in industrial clusters in the Global South included several articles by GVC scholars that dealt with CSR in industrial clusters, with foci on social upgrading (Gereffi and Lee, 2016), human rights (Giuliani, 2016), and CSR in "rising power" economies (Knorringa and Nadvi, 2016).

Yet, few contributions in economic geography and development studies have unpacked what "CSR" means in the context of GVCs. For instance, Bair and Palpacuer (2015) helpfully draw a distinction between industrial governance (coordination of actors that participate directly in GVCs) and global governance (actions of non-state actors in managing transnational processes, including norms and rules regarding global production), but do not undertake a thorough examination of how CSR is perceived by different value chain actors. Lund-Thomsen and Lindgreen (2020) also examined CSR in the GVC literature, but mainly from a buyer perspective that does not take into account how suppliers perceive CSR (Khan and Lund-Thomsen, 2011).

Furthermore, CSR definitions are not in themselves neutral. Underlying CSR definitions are particular interests of business, government, NGOs, and other stakeholders. The CSR definitions adopted by these organizations thus reflect a particular understanding of what social responsibility means in GVCs, implicitly embodying the views of some stakeholders in the value chain, while the economic, social, and environmental objectives of other stakeholders either may be overlooked or simply ignored (Blowfield and Frynas, 2005). For example, if suppliers understand CSR in different ways or perceive it as a manifestation of economic or cultural imperialism (Jammulamadaka, 2015), the misaligned expectations and intentions between buyers and suppliers likely create problems, including a risk that suppliers claim code compliance, but maintain sub-standard working conditions (Barrientos, 2019b). Accordingly, we require a better sense of how suppliers understand CSR, and the alignment between this understanding and buyers' views as encapsulated in buyers' codes of conduct (Bae et al., 2020).

In the following, I take a supplier-centered approach to answer the following research question: why are suppliers in the Global South that are integrated into GVCs often highly skeptical of CSR? I argue that CSR initiatives are frequently framed and promoted by key actors in the Global North – the home markets of global lead firms, often with little regard for the unique challenges faced by suppliers and the broader circumstances of countries in the Global South in which actual production of these goods takes place. As an alternative I set out to develop a "supplier-centered view of CSR in GVCs" by briefly reviewing and critiquing some key influential CSR definitions from the view-point of these suppliers. These are CSR definitions that have emerged in the last twenty years – a period marked by an ever-growing scholarly and media interest in labor issues in GVCs. They include the European Commission's 2001 and 2011 definitions of CSR; Porter and Kramer's notion of "shared value"; political CSR; CSR as imperialism; and, finally, CSR as "greenwashing." Based on this review, I combine key considerations of local suppliers into a brief, consolidated supplier perspective on CSR in GVCs. In this way, I seek to bridge the embryonic literature on CSR in GVCs in economy geography and development studies with key insights from the CSR/business ethics literatures.

EUROPEAN COMMISSION DEFINITIONS OF CSR

CSR definitions have developed over time, and no general consensus exists of what the term means (Rasche et al., 2017). Nevertheless, it would be fair to assert that past and current conceptualizations of CSR – as related to GVCs – have largely failed to consider the concerns of weaker value chain actors, such as suppliers and workers (Khan and Lund-Thomsen, 2011). Indeed, they have assumed that the economic, social, and environmental norms and values held by value chain actors in the Global North are fully shared by actors that either directly take part in GVCs (suppliers) or that influence the functioning of these chains in the Global South (e.g., trade unions, local NGOs, governmental actors). In order to develop this line of argument, I first analyze a number of influential CSR conceptions that have emerged in the last 20 years.

I begin by examining the European Commission's well-known (2001) definition of CSR as "a concept whereby companies integrate social and environmental concerns in their business operations and in their interaction with their stakeholders on a voluntary basis" (EC, 2001, p. 8). Given that economic considerations are critical to core business operations, we would expect the definition of CSR to include a concern with "integrating *economic*, social, and environmental concerns" into key business practices. However, the implicit assumption in this definition is that business actors operate in free, open markets where supply and demand meet through the mechanism of price. In reality, as the GVC literature clearly shows, power relations among various actors along value chains are often markedly imbalanced (Dallas et al., 2019). This means that large buyers are frequently in a position to require social and environmental improvements from suppliers that involve the latter to carry extra financial burdens (Goger, 2013; Ponte, 2019). Typically, global buyers demand year-on-year price decreases in labor-intensive value chains, such as garments, textiles, footwear, and football manufacturing (Lund-Thomsen and Nadvi, 2010b). The same buyers also demand ever-shorter lead times and tend not to be willing to share the financial burden of investing in CSR upgrading of factories in the Global South. As a consequence, in the EC definition, there is no pressure on buyers to provide financial incentives for CSR improvements by their suppliers. Instead, CSR requirements commonly become added financial burdens for suppliers at the base of GVCs (Khan et al., 2020) in ways that legitimate retailers' social and environmental record (Lebaron and Lister, 2015), but have very uneven impacts on labor issues in the Global South (Locke, 2013).

From a supplier perspective, a second concern with this approach is that companies integrate social and environmental concerns on a *voluntary basis*. However, for many suppliers, compliance with CSR codes of conduct is actually de facto *mandatory* if they wish to participate in GVCs and sell their products to large buyers, such as Nike, Adidas, Ikea, and H&M. In fact, compliance with corporate codes of conduct is a prerequisite for entering into trade relationships with these brands (Lund-Thomsen and Lindgreen, 2020). Of course, suppliers can choose not to sell their products or services to buyers that wield such power, but to assume that complying with CSR requirements when trading with these global buyers is voluntary is highly unrealistic.

I do recognize that, within the European Union, CSR debates have evolved since 2001. Indeed, in 2011, the European Union introduced a revised CSR definition, which, among other things, states, "CSR is the responsibility of enterprises for their impacts on society." This involves "maximising the creation of shared value for their owners/shareholders and for their other stakeholders and society at large." At the same time, corporations should aim at "identifying, preventing and mitigating their possible adverse impacts" (EC, 2011, p. 6).

From a supplier perspective, defining CSR as the responsibility of enterprises for their impacts on society may be auspicious, as many suppliers in GVCs can rightfully claim that they have been negatively affected by the purchasing practices of global brands. As previously mentioned, yearly price declines tend to limit the possibilities of suppliers paying their workers living wages and providing other benefits, such as job security, pensions, and unemployment insurance (Amengual et al., 2020). Ever-shorter lead times tend to push suppliers to make their workers perform overtime or engage in subcontracting to lower-tier suppliers in order to be able to meet production orders on time. Moreover, seasonal production orders make it difficult for suppliers to hire workers on longer-term contracts (Anner et al., 2013). After all, suppliers are profit-making enterprises and having workers idle on job-sites for parts of the year during the low season generates costs that they often cannot sustain. As a result, suppliers are sometimes compelled to engage in practices of labor casualization, which increase employee turnover and make it difficult for the temporary workers to have a stable income and all of the other benefits that follow from having permanent contracts (Khan et al., 2020).

The second part of the definition, which introduces Porter and Kramer's (2011) notion of "shared value," seems to imply a positive impact on suppliers and their workers, as both buyers and suppliers, as well as society (which remains undefined in Porter and Kramer's work), gain something from their GVC participation. From a supplier perspective, however, it could be argued that this "shared value" should be more equally distributed along value chains. For instance, in the production of a football, the retail price for a match ball in Europe may be approximately EUR 100. Out of this amount, a supplier in Pakistan or China is likely to receive approximately 5–8 EUR (Khan and Lund-Thomsen, 2011). In such situations, it is more accurate to claim the existence of "unequally distributed" rather than "shared" value.

Some global buyers have attempted to systematically address the negative effects of their purchasing practices on local suppliers (Amengual et al., 2020). This includes efforts at working with fewer suppliers in strategic partnerships, engaging in longer-term forecasting of demand, providing better financial incentives for engaging in CSR, and working collaboratively in training of management and workers in supplier factories (Lund-Thomsen and Lindgreen, 2020). These efforts, however, have also led the same global buyers to increasingly engage in risk management strategies, with a primary emphasis on making sure that particular human rights violations, such as the worst forms of child labor, human trafficking, and forced labor, do not take place along their value chains (Buhman et al., 2019). Such strategies often seem to be aimed at protecting the reputation of global brands (Mitkidis et al., 2019), in what *New York Times* language expert, William Safire, terms the CYA ("cover-your-ass") principle: "the bureaucratic technique of averting future accusations of policy error or wrongdoing by deflecting responsibility in advance" (Safire, 2008, p. 163). The definition's emphasis on "identifying, preventing and mitigating their possible adverse impacts" seems to imply a more risk-averse approach. In other words, brands might become pre-occupied with "looking good" rather than "doing good" for the suppliers, workers, and communities in which they are engaged in various production sites around the world – instead of taking long-term responsibility for improving the economic, social, and/or environmental conditions of production in the Global South (Lund-Thomsen, 2008).

POLITICAL CSR

More recently, a fourth perspective on CSR – *the political perspective* – has gained ground. This views firms' motivation as related to their increasingly becoming political actors that need to manage a new set of responsibilities (Rasche et al., 2017), including their role in governing GVCs (Scherer et al., 2014). According to Rasche et al. (2017, p. 276), political CSR (PCSR) is concerned with corporations striving to shape public debates and decision-making processes in a more socially and environmentally responsible manner. In particular, the political CSR perspective sees corporations as providers of public goods – frequently in the Global South – where the state has been unable or unwilling to provide these goods. Accordingly, corporations may contribute to the provision of public goods in different areas, such as public health, infrastructure, the enforcement of social and environmental standards along the value chain, or participate in the struggle against global warming, corruption, discrimination, or inequality. In political CSR, corporations are regarded as contributing to the effective resolution of such public issues, not only due to economic motivations, but also with the wider aim of enhancing social welfare ("it is the right thing to do").

While PCSR may be perceived as a normative view of what the role of multinational companies *should be* in global society (including in the regulation of GVCs), it seems quite removed from present-day de facto realities of CSR in GVCs as experienced by many suppliers in the Global South. First, while multinational companies are often involved in collective decision-making related to the enforcement of social and environmental standards (e.g., through multi-stakeholder initiatives) in cooperation with NGOs and other civil society actors, these standards have rarely been developed with substantial inputs from suppliers (or governments) in the Global South (De Bakker et al., 2019). Consequently, suppliers are often de facto excluded from collective decision-making processes in such fora. Even in instances in which they might be included, decision-making structures and the use of participatory facilitation techniques tend to only legitimate particular points of view and ways of deliberating, leading to the (unintentional) exclusion of the interests and voices of value chain participants (including those of suppliers) from the Global South (Cheyns, 2014).

Second, the idea that European and North American multinational companies should be in a position to contribute to the "effective resolution of public issues in a legitimate manner" is likely to be regarded uneasily by many suppliers and governments in the Global South. From a supplier perspective, "public issues" tend to refer to those issues that are of immediate interest to Western consumers (e.g., the eradication of child labor) and not those of interest to suppliers and/or workers, such as increasing business volume, offering better prices, creating additional jobs, and/or improving worker incomes and skills training (Khan and Lund-Thomsen, 2011).

Moreover, the legitimacy of multinational companies in the "effective resolution of public issues" may also be called into question. In the 1990s, governments – along with some trade unions – from the Global South refused to have labor standards incorporated as part of the World Trade Organization's mandate. As a result, many European and North American activists began focusing on multinational companies, pressuring them to include social and environmental standards in their GVCs. From the supplier perspective, this could be perceived as European and North American CSR activists bypassing governments in the Global South, and using GVCs as a way of "sneaking in" labor and environmental standards through the backdoor of interfirm linkages that include large transnational firms and local suppliers (Knight and Greenberg, 2002).

CSR AS IMPERIALISM AND GREENWASHING

Such views of CSR are by no means unique amongst manufacturers in the Global South. In fact, suppliers in the Global South sometimes contend that CSR is a thinly veiled attempt at re-introducing age-old colonialist ideals, and economic and cultural imperialism of yesteryear (Jammulamadaka, 2015). Essentially, the definition of CSR as imperialism understands CSR as a process through which "economic resources are extracted from local manufacturers while their perceptions of what constitutes socially responsible behaviour are delegitimized" (Khan and Lund-Thomsen, 2011, p. 73). This viewpoint, that is, "CSR as imperialism," is vividly related in Ali Khan's (2007) book, *Representing Children*, in which an exporter from the Sialkot football manufacturing cluster describes his experience with international buyers that are keen to eliminate child labor from the industry. According to the exporter, the West employs double standards when it enforces programs aimed at eliminating child labor from the industry. In his view, countries in the Global North managed to develop their own nations. However, when it comes to countries in the Global South, countries in the Global North want to keep their Southern counterparts in a strait jacket. Indeed, the exporter sees it as ironic that the United States should care about the plight of children in Pakistan, when the United States has its own history of genocide and slavery. In fact, he relates that when he asks his buyers to pay higher prices for his company's products, they do not wish to make concessions in the rates they pay to his company. It is critical to note that the argument here is in no way in favor of child labor or exploitation of any sort to justify economic development. On the contrary, the argument is that exploitation and other severely deleterious practices at the supply level are tightly connected to the commercial practices of global buyers in the North (see also Barrientos, 2019b).

From a supplier perspective, global buyers are also thought to be pushing CSR along value chains to enroll producers in "greenwashing" of their global sourcing operations. Corpwatch, a critical NGO, defines greenwashing as "the phenomenon of socially and environmentally destructive corporations attempting to preserve and expand their markets by posing as friends of the environment and leaders in the struggle against poverty" (Corpwatch, 2020). Here, global buyers will emphasize the detection of violations of minimum standards related to wages, work hours, and occupational health and safety, since this focus provides them with legitimacy and serves as a shield against the reputational risks created by advocacy campaigns. Simultaneously, however, these buyers will often deemphasize the rights of workers to form independent trade unions and engage in collective bargaining, as this diminishes managerial control of the GVC and provides few reputational benefits (Anner, 2012). However, from a supplier perspective, if multinational companies were truly concerned about ensuring better labor and environmental conditions in their value chains, they would source products or establish factories in their home countries, where wages are much higher and where the enforcement of labor legislation is likely to be far stricter than it is in countries, such as India or Pakistan.

For many suppliers, global buyers spend a lot of time and energy on their commitments to CSR in discursive terms, but in practice outsource much of their production to low-wage countries in order to be able to reap larger profits on their own. Indeed, it is the case that the labor and environmental costs of operating such factories in European or North American contexts would likely be so high that they would be financially unviable.

A SUPPLIER PERSPECTIVE ON CSR IN GVCS

Drawing on this brief review of recent CSR definitions, I now combine some of these supplier considerations in a more consolidated supplier perspective on CSR in GVCs. This supplier perspective on CSR in GVCs implies that power imbalances in GVCs between buyers and suppliers place severe constraints on what suppliers can do in relation to integrating social and environmental concerns in their business operations and interaction with other actors (cf. EC, 2001 definition of CSR). Price declines, seasonal demand changes, shorter lead times, payment delays, and buyer unwillingness to co-finance CSR upgradation leave suppliers in a very tight financial situation if they want to address CSR concerns at the factory level. Yet, if they are selling into high-value markets in Europe and North America, they are nevertheless compelled to comply with buyer-driven CSR demands. At the same time, even if suppliers can identify the "possible adverse impacts" (cf. EC, 2011 CSR definition) of their business activities (e.g., overtime and subcontracting into the informal economy), it becomes highly challenging for suppliers to mitigate and address these impacts, which are to a large extent driven by buyer purchasing practices.

In the supplier perspective on CSR in GVCs, there is thus little "shared value" (cf. Porter and Kramer, 2011 notion), as CSR mainly appears to bring reputational benefits to brands/retailers, but few economic, social, or environmental benefits to suppliers. From the supplier perspective, CSR may thus not only constitute a kind of economic imperialism, as retailers and brands extract profits from suppliers and workers at the base of the GVC, but their CSR demands are often perceived as a kind of cultural imperialism by suppliers (cf. Khan and Lund-Thomsen, 2011 definition). For instance, if retailers/brands demand that young workers between the ages of 15 and 17 must not labor in export-oriented industries, this might prevent these workers from learning a new skill and entering an occupation, such as football stitching. This could, in turn, lead to labor shortages over time, threatening the future viability of an industry, such as football manufacturing, in Pakistan or India (Lund-Thomsen, 2008).

Furthermore, if the intention behind CSR activities is to help to provide public goods in areas, such as Decent Work, where states in the Global South have not been able to (cf. political CSR definition), suppliers are not only severely financially constrained in their ability to do so, but they may also wind up, for instance, in order not to be seen as employing child workers, engaging in interventions that leave these workers worse off. An example of this would be firing child workers in garment factories, who are then relegated to working in much worse occupations, such as child prostitution (Husselbee, 2000).

From the supplier perspective on CSR in GVCs, addressing these challenges calls for equal sharing of the profits generated through the sales of the products that they manufacture for end markets in the Global North. This necessitates a reform of trading relations that secure long-term cooperation between buyers and suppliers, more stable production forecasting and planning, avoidance of last minute orders, increasing lead times for production, incorporating the costs of CSR upgradation in product prices, and ensuring that particular CSR requirements are made with due reference to local socio-economic and socio-cultural realities. This should be done in order to ensure that CSR requirements do not create unintended negative consequences for the local workforce and the environment in the Global South.

CONCLUSION

In this chapter, I argued that CSR definitions are often articulated and advocated by actors in the Global North in ways that ignore the unique challenges and circumstances faced by suppliers and countries in the Global South. Instead, I suggest that CSR in GVCs must be understood in relation to what stage in the GVC it is applied, and the institutional context in which it is embedded. For instance, the role of trade unions in CSR will differ between countries, such as India, where some trade unions are linked directly to different political parties (e.g., Congress and the Communist party), and China, where the Communist-party-backed All China Federation of Trade Unions is the country's sole legally mandated trade union.

In doing so, I am not arguing that I am in agreement with what I have described here as a supplier-centered perspective on CSR in GVCs. In fact, suppliers have sometimes engaged in irresponsible practices, such as breaking up trade unions, or employing forced labor or prison labor in GVCs. Instead, at a time when almost all large multinational companies claim to work with CSR in GVCs, my intervention should be seen as a caution against the Eurocentric domination of CSR conceptions, and the assumption that it makes sense for Global North corporations and governments to define what CSR is from their point of view and then seek to implement that through GVCs in ways that lead to the reinforcement of highly unequal distributions of trading relations. Indeed, we now need to go beyond poorly conceived imaginations of what might be socially relevant ways of addressing labor rights and environmental issues in the Global South. In the next chapter, I move on to examine what one such more "Southern-centered" perspective on supplier responsibility in GVCs may look like. I do this by exploring the potential and limitations of collective supplier engagement in CSR in industrial clusters that are tied into GVCs in the Global South.

4. Cluster-centered perspectives

INTRODUCTION

In economic geography and development studies, there has been a long-standing tradition of discussing how local economic regions, also known as industrial clusters, can ensure more stable, long-term gains from their participation in GVCs (Schmitz and Nadvi, 1999; Knorringa and Nadvi, 2016). Industrial clusters can here be defined as "geographical concentrations of firms and ancillary units engaged in the same sector" (Nadvi and Barrientos, 2004, p. V). The answer has generally been seen as one of economic upgrading where local suppliers produce better products, more efficiently, move into more value-added functions in the chain and use skills learned from competing in one industry to gain competitive advantage in other industries (Humphrey and Schmitz, 2002, Schmitz, 2006). However, more recently, it has become increasingly apparent that such forms of economic upgrading do not automatically translate into *social upgrading* – "the process of improvement in the rights and entitlements of workers as social actors, which enhances the quality of their employment" (Barrientos et al., 2011, p. 323).[1]

In fact, this trend applies particularly to women workers in industrial clusters (UNIDO, 2019). In recent years, employment in some clusters in the Global South has become heavily feminized, for instance, reaching beyond 90% amongst factory-based women clothing stitchers in the garment clusters of South India (Mezzadri and Fan, 2018). At the same time, such feminized forms of employment in industrial clusters are often insecure, unsafe, and poorly paid (Lund-Thomsen, 2013), characterized by long working hours, a lack of collective bargaining/freedom of association, and sexual harassment in the workplace (Mezzadri, 2014a, 2014b). In short, women workers are typically exposed to higher levels of material poverty, face greater levels of gender discrimination in and beyond the workplace, and greater inequality in relation to the types and conditions of employment in industrial clusters in the Global South than they are likely to do in industrial clusters in the Global North (UNIDO, 2019).

Added to this are the particular risks faced by women workers when industrial clusters are tied into GVCs (UNIDO, 2019). In fact, the global capitalist economy has sometimes been compared to a boom and bust economy (Werner and Bair, 2019). During times of economic growth, increased consumption in the Global North creates millions of jobs for workers in various producer countries around the world, while migrants move from rural areas into cities in search of work (Bair and Werner, 2011). However, as the international health crisis related to the spread of COVID-19 has illustrated, the gains obtained for local export-oriented enterprises and workers from their participation in GVCs linking consumers and brands in the Global North with dispersed producers in the Global South have often been short-lived (Oka et al., 2020a). For example, in Bangladesh alone, an estimated two million workers were at risk of losing their main source of income as production came to a halt in the spring of 2020. In fact, some workers and their families were at the point of facing starvation as a result of COVID-19 (Anner, 2020). Moreover, this global boom and bust approach to global economic organization has a particular gender slant – often with women being employed in more temporary, lower-skilled, and less paid jobs, thus placing them in a particularly vulnerable position when the global economy contracts (Barrientos, 2019a).

This is what I coin "the devil's deal"[2] for women laboring in industrial clusters that are tied into GVCs in the Global South. In short, paradoxically, although local producer insertion in GVCs might facilitate local economic growth processes in industrial clusters, this could also simultaneously result in social downgrading of women workers in the same local regions (Lund-Thomsen and Coe, 2015). Hence, women workers will often be more vulnerable to economic restructuring and social downgrading than men in industrial clusters in the Global South (UNIDO, 2019).

On the one hand, there is now a long-standing tradition of academic research on the social upgrading and downgrading of women workers in GVCs (Barrientos, 2019a, 2019b; Barrientos et al., 2003; Prieto-Carron, 2006; Tallontire et al., 2005). On the other hand, academic work that *conceptualizes* the gendered nature of social upgrading and downgrading in *industrial clusters* is virtually absent (Pyke and Lund-Thomsen, 2016). Authors such as Gereffi and Lee (2016) have sought to theorize the role of private, public, and social governance in facilitating the social upgrading (but not downgrading) of workers in cluster settings, but without adopting a particular gender angle to their work. Knorringa and Nadvi (2016) have touched upon the role of so-called local "social contracts" whereby the private sector, public authorities, and civil society actors reach an informal agreement or settlement that define the prospects (and limitations) for social upgrading in industrial clusters in Rising Power economies. Moreover, authors such as Lund-Thomsen and Nadvi (2010b) and Lund-Thomsen et al. (2016) have sought to conceptualize how GVC governance and local industrial cluster governance interact in enabling the engagement of local suppliers in corporate social responsibility

(CSR) activities, but without adopting a particular angle on the gendered nature of social upgrading and downgrading in cluster settings.

Hence, a critical question becomes: *under what circumstances might laboring in industrial clusters in the Global South enhance and/or undermine the social upgrading of women workers? What is the scope for collective supplier engagement in CSR to socially upgrade the work conditions of women workers in these clusters?* These are the questions that I seek to answer in this chapter.

The chapter proceeds as follows. First, I discuss key conceptual insights from the literature on the gendered nature of social upgrading and downgrading in GVCs. I then analyze how the gendered nature of industrial organization within mature clusters is likely to result in an overall trajectory of social downgrading amongst women workers. I argue that cluster integration into GVCs will not simply disrupt the gendered nature of industrial organization within mature clusters. In fact, the integration of mature clusters in GVCs will likely re-articulate existing gender inequalities and disparities in local economic regions in ways that enable the efficient functioning and exploitative functioning of GVCs. Third, I argue that joint action CSR initiatives amongst multiple actors within mature clusters have limited potential to overcome such structurally embedded and gendered inequalities. Finally, in the conclusion, I summarize and critically examine the main limitations of this line of argument, outlining a future research agenda on the interface between GVCs, industrial clusters, and women's social upgrading and downgrading in the Global South.

INDUSTRIAL CLUSTERS AND THE GENDERED NATURE OF SOCIAL UP/DOWNGRADING

I start out by looking at the notion of industrial clusters itself – a concept which is highly disputed in its own right. In fact, the term "industrial cluster" is often used indiscriminately for a broad range of business arrangements which, in fact, may be used to describe local concentrations of certain economic activities in a very broad sense (Altenburg and Meyer-Stamer, 1999). Hence, different cluster typologies have also been developed in the context of the Global South. For instance, Schmitz and Nadvi (1999) distinguish between "incipient" clusters – those at an early stage of industrial development, usually located in poor areas, producing for local markets with simple technologies and labor skills, and "mature" clusters – relatively more advanced in terms of technology and skills, often producing for global markets and thus vulnerable to global competitive pressures.

Another categorization of industrial clusters in the Global South was introduced by Altenburg and Meyer-Stamer (1999) who distinguish between "survival" clusters, "advanced mass production"[3] clusters, and "clusters of transnational corporations."[4] Their notion of "survival" clusters is similar to

Schmitz and Nadvi's "incipient" clusters. Such clusters are in "poor areas, where open or disguised unemployment is high, either in small towns of rural areas or on the outskirts of big cities." In a third conception, Sandee (2002) distinguishes between "dormant" clusters at one end – manufacturing simple items for poor rural consumers and providing "distress" employment for those with limited income generating options, and "dynamic" clusters at the other end – where firms are closely networked and can enter wider, even global, markets.

A key argument here is that only mature industrial clusters will have the types of industrial cluster features that make cluster integration into GVCs possible, thus enabling and/or undermining the social upgrading of women workers as they participate in the world economy. Schmitz and Nadvi (1999) described these as clusters that were relatively more advanced in terms of technology usage and skills than survival or dormant clusters, typically producing for export-markets and thus subject to global competition. In mature clusters, the critical challenge for local firms inserted in GVCs is to produce at scale, with standardized products, deliver these products on time, and comply with social and environmental standards (Lund-Thomsen et al., 2012).

Beyond highlighting that only mature clusters will likely be able to sell into demanding GVCs, I also argue that the main features of industrial clustering are likely to have implications for women's social upgrading and downgrading. I summarize these as follows:

i.   First, industrial clusters include agglomeration benefits that generate economies of scale and scope for small clustered producers. These include economic externalities that arise from the presence of a critical mass of firms, suppliers, and a skilled labor pool within the confines of the cluster, as well as through flows of information, knowledge, and skills within the cluster (Gulati et al., 2018).

ii.   Second, small producers, through clustering are able to overcome many of the limitations imposed upon them by their size. In addition, clustering offers the possibility for local joint action. This can result in competitive advantages for clustered producers that lie beyond their capacities as individual producers (Giuliani, 2016).

iii. Third, joint action, however, is not a necessary outcome of clustering, and can be very difficult to motivate especially where firms primarily compete with each other. Nevertheless, where joint action takes place, gains to cluster-based actors can be significant. This often arises in the face of external shocks where, through joint action and cooperation, local firms find ways to confront common challenges (Nadvi, 2016).

In short, the prospects for mature industrial clusters to enhance and/or undermine women's social upgrading is closely related to two factors: the geographical proximity of firms and joint action between local firms and institutions within the cluster. I deal with each of these in turn below.

The Proximity of Cluster-Based Firms

First, it is clear that an agglomeration of firms in the same locality can create particular structural conditions that influence the scope for women's social upgrading and downgrading in local economic regions. Hence, a concentration of job options and skills upgrading point in the direction of the gendered nature of social upgrading opportunities. For instance, industrial clustering may be associated with highly gendered work patterns that are particularly dominant. For example, De Neve (2014) argues that young, unmarried, female migrant workers have migrated to the city of Tiruppur, India in search of work where they now labor in factories according to a 9–5 work routine. Thus, in Indian garment clusters, Mezzadri (2016) highlights that gendered wage differentials in factories have worked as a powerful recruiting device for firms in Indian industrial clusters. "Troublesome" male workers have been possible to replace with more "docile" and "loving" female labor. Mezzadri (2014a) thus notes that wage differentials in factory-based settings are reinforced through the social construction of skills. This supports the broader contention of feminist scholars that occupations – and here subsequent *social downgrading processes* – are constructed through gender ideologies (Elson and Pearson, 1981; Munir et al., 2018).

Second, community norms and values amongst cluster entrepreneurs and workers can lead to a concentration of women workers in jobs that are socially downgraded. As Nadvi (1999) argues, social networks, based on kinships, family, and localness, influence production relations within clusters, and the influence of such networks change over time. In this regard, the maintenance of a skilled and specialized local workforce is critically dependent on the sphere of social reproduction (Nadvi and Barrientos, 2004). For instance, in the case of the Sialkot football manufacturing cluster, Khan (Khan, A., 2007) describes how women football workers in the cluster were able to combine home-based stitching with taking care of their children and household duties simultaneously. The dominant, patriarchal values and norms amongst their male family members emphasized that these women could only work at home, and not outside in factories, as this might mean that they might be harassed, have relationships with men, or engage in sexual conduct in ways that would compromise their family's honor. Hence, such norms and values could be seen as facilitating *social downgrading*, denying women workers access to better paid work with higher levels of social protection outside of the home sphere.

Third, job-hopping options in geographically concentrated labor markets within clusters permit women workers to opt in and out of jobs, combining work in the commercial sphere with social reproduction in the household sphere (Lund-Thomsen, 2013). Typically, this will largely be compatible with a trajectory towards *social downgrading* for women workers in mature industrial clusters. For example, Knorringa (1999), in his analysis of the Agra footwear cluster in India, describes how the cluster is internationally com-petitive, because of its skilled, artisanal labor that is not only cheap but also abundantly available. This means that first-tier entrepreneurs in the cluster can call upon these workers at an instant's notice, with skilled artisans frequently moving between one workshop and another, sometimes playing alternate roles as piece-rate factory workers, unpaid family laborers, and being in charge of their own home-based units. On the one hand, this constitutes a path towards *social downgrading* – that is, workers receiving very low salaries, having unstable employment, low levels or complete absence of social protection. At the same time, the frequent changes in employment make it very challenging for workers to collectively organize and join trade unions.

However, even if the overall trajectory is towards social downgrading, there may still be some space for women's labor agency in mature industrial clusters, although this is likely to be highly constrained (Lund-Thomsen and Coe, 2015). For instance, De Neve (2014) thus describes how employment in informal sector workshops in the Tiruppur garment cluster permitted married women with young children to both take care of their home-based duties including child-rearing while working flexible hours, quitting and rejoining particular workshops, in relation to their broader life circumstances. This may enable women workers to exercise greater agency in terms of entering or exiting different workplaces in accordance with their broader life circum-stances. In short, I would still argue that even if only low-skilled, poorly paid jobs may be available for women workers in mature industrial clusters, these clusters may still offer job options for minimum income generation in ways that are compatible with their work in the sphere of social reproduction.

Fourth, and relatedly, industrial clustering enables collective action amongst workers that is gendered in nature (dominated by men); in ways that promote social upgrading opportunities for men but not women. For instance, in the Sialkot and Jalandhar football clusters in Pakistan and India, skilled, male artisans tended to stitch footballs within formal factory settings until the early 1970s (Lund-Thomsen and Nadvi, 2010b). At the time, international demand started increasing from global buyers, mainly in Europe and North America, leading to an expansion of the workforce, and increased trade union activity, particularly in Pakistan at a time when the government of Zulfiqar Ali Bhutto was trying to promote workers' rights across the country. Here trade union activity was facilitated by the close geographical proximity of enterprises within these cities (Khan, A., 2007). However, the options for such joint action amongst workers to result in social upgrading are in themselves highly gendered as trade unions in the Global South are often male dominated, advocating the demands of their male members and (perhaps unintendedly) sidelining the particular concerns and voices of women workers in industrial clusters (Khara and Lund-Thomsen, 2012).

Fifth, the agglomeration of firms in industrial clusters also creates particular structural conditions for gendered social upgrading and downgrading to the extent that clusters are home to geographical concentrations of "hidden", subcontracted value chains that lead to social downgrading – particularly of women and child workers (Lund-Thomsen and Nadvi, 2010b). In fact, the flexibility, specialized division of labor between firms, and the extensive use of subcontracting has traditionally been described as a source of local economic competitiveness in the industrial cluster literature (Becattini, 1990, Pyke et al., 1990). However, international media reports have often reported on labor rights violations in "hidden, subcontracted supply chains" including the use of child labor and more vulnerable women workers. For instance, the Sialkot surgical instruments cluster was exposed to negative international media attention in the 1990s, including the involvement of child labor and poor conditions for women workers in the industry's "hidden" subcontracted value chains (Junaid et al., 2017).

Finally, the agglomeration of firms within one locality may also matter for gendered social upgrading and downgrading patterns depending upon the *types of work* available within these local labor markets. Barrientos et al. (2011) thus make a useful distinction between different types of work. These authors distinguish between the following categories of work: (i) small-scale, household work. This type of work is typically performed by small-scale producers or outgrowers involved in agricultural production, and homeworkers in more labor-intensive or artisanal types of manufacturing; (ii) low-skilled, labor-intensive work. This relates to the use of wage labor in a formal factory setting, often involving wage employment between an employer (who may be the producer or an agent) and a worker (normally paid in cash, but sometimes in kind); (iii) medium-skilled, mixed production technologies work. This has to do with skilled workers capable not only of making key components and finished products, but also of performing production-related service jobs like product design, quality control, packing and logistics, which require a broad range of skills; (iv) high-skilled, technology-intensive work. This relates to workers being able to perform high-skilled work in capital- and technology-intensive industries, such as automobiles and electronics, often for mega-suppliers to Western brands; and (v) knowledge-intensive work. This typically arises from the outsourcing of services and involves more advanced business services such as finance, accounting, software, medical services, and engineering.

In mature clusters, in industries such as garments, textiles, leather, or footwear manufacturing, the vast majority of job opportunities will mainly be concentrated in the areas of small-scale, household work or low-skilled labor-intensive work which tend to be dominated by women workers (Lund-Thomsen et al., 2016). Hence, the geographical proximity of local firms in these types of clusters typically present options for women's *social upgrading* in terms of expanding the *quantity* of jobs available to women. However, simultaneously, industrial clustering here also presents some structural limitations to women's social upgrading. In fact, in these types of work, the *quality* of jobs available tend to involve very low wages and poor occupational health and safety, as well as lack of social protection which could generally be seen as trends towards *social downgrading*.

CLUSTERS, CHAINS, AND WOMEN'S SOCIAL DOWNGRADING: THE DEVIL'S DEAL

How does the insertion of mature industrial clusters into GVCs then affect the prospects for social up/downgrading of women workers within these local economic settings? Unlike the industrial cluster literature where the gendered nature of social up/downgrading remains underexplored, there has been a substantial literature that has analyzed the gendered nature of social upgrading and downgrading in GVCs in the last twenty years (Tallontire et al., 2005; Prieto-Carron, 2006, 2008; Mezzadri, 2014a; 2014b; Said-Allsopp and Tallontire, 2015; Ruwanpura and Hughes, 2016; McCarthy and Moon, 2018; Barrientos, 2019a, 2019b; McCarthy et al., 2020). Empirically, a lot of attention has been directed to exploring how global retail value chains are shaping gendered patterns of work, and what the gendered outcomes are for workers. This includes analyses of how retail value chains have changed in the last twenty-five years, how these are socially embedded, and how gendered boundaries are shifting between the spheres of commercial production and social reproduction (Barrientos, 2019b). In fact, the gendered nature of social upgrading/downgrading in GVCs appears to be mediated by at least three different factors: (a) the specificity of value chains/industry dynamics in different sectors; (b) the national institutional contexts in which GVCs touch down; and (c) their dynamic interaction over time (Lund-Thomsen and Coe, 2015; Barrientos, 2019b).

Thus, the dynamic interaction of specific value chains and institutional contexts mediate issues such as implicit and explicit discrimination; physical, verbal and sexual harassment; occupational segregation; and pay gaps as well as legal and cultural barriers (such as particular laws, patriarchy and family/kinship patterns) that prevent women from participating in economic, social, and political life (Barrientos, 2019a). The literature explains how such inequalities exist due to the social construction and performativity of gender categories (Kabeer, 2000; Butler, 2006), rather than biological sex.

In this section of the chapter, I argue that – in the case of gender – the insertion of mature industrial clusters into GVCs does not build so much on the *disarticulation* of previously existing economic structures within industrial clusters but rather on a *re-articulation* of pre-existing gender inequalities to the benefit of exploitative functioning of GVCs. I suggest that these previously existing structures include: (i) firm agglomeration in the same geographical place; (ii) community norms and values amongst entrepreneurs and workers; (iii) job hopping in geographically concentrated labor markets; (iv) collective organization amongst workers; (iv) subcontracted value chains; and (v) the types of work available within the cluster.

I seek inspiration from the so-called disarticulations perspective on GVCs (Bair and Werner, 2011; Bair et al., 2013; Werner and Bair, 2019). The disarticulations perspective starts from the observation that there has been an inclusionary bias in GVC studies. In other words, there has been a focus on how actors and places such as suppliers, farmers, and workers as well as local economic regions more generally benefit from or are disenfranchised due to their inclusion in GVCs (Bair and Werner, 2011). Instead the disarticulations perspective suggests that GVCs are not only shaped by geographies (for instance, local economic regions) but they also reshape these geographies over time. Hence, the concept of disarticulations highlights the disruptions, instabilities, and provisional outsides of GVCs (Bair et al., 2013). In other words, the constantly shifting boundaries of GVCs will not only include particular actors and places, but also exclude some actors and places over time (Gutelius, 2015). Hence, the disarticulations perspective describes these exclusion processes through terms such as devaluation, regional disinvestment, and constitutive exclusions.

I will now try to look at the integration of mature industrial clusters into GVCs through this analytical lens. My argument proceeds as follows. First, if mature clusters are increasingly integrated into GVCs, this may lead to a re-articulation, a strengthening, and deepening of pre-existing, particularly gendered work patterns in the cluster. For instance, increased availability of job options in South Asian industrial clusters may attract young women migrant workers who are socially constructed as more "docile" than "aggressive male workers" and thus willing to accept working for lower wages in factories than male counterparts. Hence, increased export-orientation in the cluster may – while leading to a short-term expansion of jobs for women workers – also likely lead to an intensification of socially constructed and gendered social downgrading processes for women workers.

Second, the increased integration of mature industrial clusters into GVCs may also be facilitated by particular community norms and values that result in women workers laboring in jobs that are socially downgraded. For instance, if community norms and values emphasize that women should mainly take care of children and perform household duties, an expansion of production to meet demand in export-markets, given the high volatility of global demand, may lead to a concentration of women in second, third, or fourth value chain tiers within the cluster. These women can then be called upon to meet short-term demands, but it often leaves the women with fluctuating incomes and lower levels of protection than if they had been employed in first-tier, "front-line" factories. Conversely, these women are particularly vulnerable if global buyers decide to disengage from particular clusters. Not only do they likely enter the workforce in the lowest paid jobs, they will also lose this mediocre source of income if the cluster loses its international customers.

Third, as a mature cluster increasingly is inserted into a GVC, job-hopping options within clusters likely increase, giving women increased options for combining work in the commercial sphere with social reproduction in the household sphere. This may lead to an intensification of social downgrading processes. In other words, more job-hopping options are accompanied by more women workers receiving low salaries, suffering from unstable employment and incomes, and very low levels of social protection. With ever-expanding production as buyer demands increase, and a larger number of workers shifting between jobs in different factories/workshops, the dynamic nature of mature cluster integration into GVCs makes it ever more challenging to collective organize, defend, and improve their work conditions in these chains. This likely becomes even more challenging if international buyers subsequently exit the cluster.

Fourth, as mature clusters integrate further into GVCs, the increased number and concentration of workers within a confined geographical space may also spur more strikes and worker attempts at organizing themselves. However, attempts at enabling collective action amongst workers may further aggravate gender inequalities to the extent that existing trade unions tend to be highly male dominated. If their scope for action increases as part of a mature cluster integration into GVCs, it also means that the voices of male workers will likely come to dominate industrial action even more, while the voices of women workers – even if they increasingly form part of the cluster workforce – may be further marginalized. Conversely, if global buyers decide to exit from a mature industrial cluster, the gendered nature of worker organizing within these clusters mean that women workers may likely also have the least voice in terms of influencing social downgrading processes. For instance, they may have the least influence regarding the (sometimes illegal) lay-off of workers, the payment of due wages, unemployment insurance, and pension benefits.

Fifth, if mature industrial clusters step up their participation in GVCs, the need for supplier flexibility, specialized division of labor between firms, and subcontracting within the cluster will likely also increase. Hence, while mature clusters often survive and prosper through these combined sources of competitiveness during GVC participation, it also leads to risks associated with the increased use of child labor, forced labor, and exploitation of women workers in "hidden" value chains. In short, cluster integration into GVCs is likely associated with an increasing trend towards social downgrading. Conversely, while buyers exiting from mature industrial clusters may remove some of these "hidden" value chains, their removal from the cluster may simply mean that these marginalized parts of the cluster workforce, including home-based women workers, go from having a very meager income to having no income at all accruing from their value chain participation.

Finally, cluster expansion into value chains is in turn accompanied by the creation of particular types of jobs. In South Asian garments, textiles, leather, or footwear clusters, most new job opportunities will be created in small-scale, household work or low-skilled labor-intensive work that are typically dominated by women workers. In the short term, mature cluster integration into GVCs may enhance social upgrading options by increasing the numbers of jobs available to women in the cluster. However, the quality of these new jobs will likely provide them with poverty-level wages, increased occupational health and safety risks, and an absence of social protection mechanisms.

To sum up, the participation of mature South Asian industrial clusters in the garments, textiles, leather, and footwear GVCs reinforces "the devil's deal": even though local industrial clusters may experience economic growth and increased export-orientation, the outcome of cluster integration into GVCs is a trend towards social downgrading for women workers that labor in these local economic regions.

COLLECTIVE CSR ACTION IN INDUSTRIAL CLUSTERS

I now turn to the role of CSR involving cooperation between local cluster-based firms and related support institutions such as business associations, universities, technical institutes, and public sector agencies. Building on my earlier work on social upgrading and downgrading in industrial clusters in the Global South (see e.g., Lund-Thomsen and Nadvi, 2010b; Pyke and Lund-Thomsen, 2016; Lund-Thomsen et al., 2016), I limit my focus to *buyer-driven GVCs* characterized by low entry barriers for new producers and low technology requirements for engaging in production (Gereffi, 2019), and *mature, labor-intensive export-oriented clusters* where the potential for social upgrading and downgrading of women workers in industrial clusters is particularly acute, given the large number of women workers involved in these export-oriented clusters (UNIDO, 2019). This includes clusters in the global garment, footwear, and leather manufacturing industries that sell into *high end markets* in Europe and the United States where consumers are more likely to care about the social upgrading and social downgrading of women workers at the base of GVCs in the Global South (Lund-Thomsen and Lindgreen, 2020).

In regional terms, I zoom in on *South Asia* given that most of the world's industrial clusters are located in this region, and that levels of gender inequality in South Asia are considered to be highest in the world. Moreover, industrial clusters found in this region have particular features that are likely to be different from more modern, highly mechanized industrial clusters that may be in countries such as China (Knorringa and Nadvi, 2016). Particular features of South Asian clusters include (a) work often taking place in home-based units with female labor, (b) workshops managed by white-collar traders/ entrepreneurs that pay piece rates and often subcontract labor recruitment to master-artisans; and (c) only a very limited number of relatively larger export-oriented firms in high-profile consumer-facing sectors like garments and footwear that offer labor contracts to workers (Lund-Thomsen et al., 2016). Although most workers are not offered formal contracts, they are clearly not an anonymous mass (Knorringa and Nadvi, 2016). As Mezzadri (2014a) argues, intricate relations of patronage, debt, and social obligation exist in a highly exploitative local labor markets. Seasonal production patterns and the dominant piece-rate system effectively means that workers labor in a highly volatile fashion within these clusters (Mezzadri, 2014b).

Within these cluster and value chain contexts, I argue that CSR initiatives could both have positive and negative, intended and unintended consequences for women's social upgrading and downgrading. First, local firms could work with government actors, international agencies, NGOs (particularly women's NGOs) in social upgrading initiatives (Grosser, 2016), local feminist social movements (Grosser and McCarthy, 2018), and other actors in ensuring the *social upgrading* of women workers in industrial clusters. For instance, governmental actors and institutions often operate at a variety of scales ranging from the global to the local. For example, in the 2000s in the coir cluster at Alleppey, India, a global actor, United National Industrial Development Organization, intervened in a local cluster that included 45,000 spinners, most of whom were women (FMC, 2006). Here household spinning units were organized into consortia and self-help groups with the aim of securing access to finance. These networks were provided with training in marketing and improved input sourcing linkages. In the handloom cluster of Chanderi, the formation of seven self-help groups consisting of approximately 70 weavers resulted in the creation of a new organization called Bunkar Vikas Sansthan which, according to UNIDO, was able to attract repeat orders from customers such as FabIndia (FMC, 2006).

However, it is also important to recognize that joint action in industrial clusters in the Global South can also be a source of social downgrading for women workers. In fact, this depends on the type of joint action that – for instance – local firms engage in (Jamali et al., 2017). For instance, in the Sialkot football manufacturing cluster in the early 1970s, the city's football entrepreneurs decided to deal with rising labor activism and work stoppages by sending skilled, male artisans home to nearby villages, thus creating a pool of subcontractors that could transport the football panels and thread to the home-based stitchers and bring back the stitched footballs to the city-based factories. This also led to the creation of an informal, flexible workforce of home-based women workers that could be called upon in response to changing international demand patterns (Khan, F., 2007). In the football manufacturing cluster of Jalandhar, India, the decision to create a largely informal workforce in a similar way was primarily related to the entrepreneurs' wish to evade Indian labor laws that would grant the status of permanent employment to all workers in units that employed more than one hundred laborers. In both clusters, this facilitated the entry of women, home-based workers, often with very little formal education, and sometimes also child workers in the process of football stitching (Jamali et al., 2017).

CONCLUSION

In combining insights from the gendered nature of GVC and industrial cluster analysis, I argued that the insertion of mature industrial clusters into GVCs is not only likely to lead to the *disarticulation* of previously existing economic structures within these clusters but also – in the case of gender – to a *re-articulation* of pre-existing gender inequalities to the benefit of exploit-ative functioning of GVCs. I suggest that these previously existing structures include: (i) firm agglomeration in the same geographical place; (ii) community norms and values amongst entrepreneurs and workers; (iii) job hopping in geo-graphically concentrated labor markets; (iv) collective organization amongst workers; (v) subcontracted value chains; and (vi) the types of work available within the cluster.

Following the above discussion a number of themes appear as important for future research in terms of the relationship between value chains, industrial clusters, and the social up/downgrading of women workers in local economic regions in the Global South. First, it is important to go beyond the classical model of Gereffi et al. (2005) who theorized value chain governance in the relationship between global buyers and first-tier suppliers. In other words, value chain governance also needs to refer to how first-tier suppliers may become "lead firms" themselves within the cluster in terms of governing relationships with second-tier, third-tier or even fourth-tier suppliers with associated implications for women's social upgrading and downgrading.

Second, while I focus on mature industrial clusters and not incipient/survival clusters, it may well be that other types of joint action could be witnessed amongst small-scale local producers or artisans within the latter clusters (Nadvi, 2016). For instance, in countries such as India and Brazil, there have been long-established traditions of establishing cooperatives or organizational forms, such as producer companies or self-help groups, that seek to organize small-scale producers or individual workers and help them in accessing inputs such as credit, technology, know-how, and/or forms of services to improve their business potential and ensure the social upgrading of women workers at the same time (Reed and McMurtry, 2009). Hence, conceptualizing the gendered nature of social up/downgrading in incipient/survival clusters in the Global South would seem an important analytical task.

Third, as GVC actors, Southern-based lead firms may have different priorities than lead firms in Northern Europe and the United States that tend to be protecting their brand reputation in relation to current trends regarding "sustainable and socially responsible" production (Guarin and Knorringa, 2014). If Southern lead firms source on the basis of price, quality, and delivery conditions without paying attention to social and environmental concerns, this could reinforce the current trend towards social downgrading of women workers as an outcome of such trading relationships. Yet we have very little knowledge about this question.

A final issue that demands attention in future research on this topic is the role played by producer-driven value chains that have higher entry barriers and are dominated by more technology- and capital-intensive producers – for instance, in the electronics or airline manufacturing industries (Lund-Thomsen and Lindgreen, 2018). For example, if the types of work undertaken in electronics industry clusters are mainly related to medium-skilled, mixed production technologies work or high-skilled, technology-intensive work, the prospects for women's social upgrading might be better in such clusters than in industrial clusters that are tied into buyer-driven value chains (see also, Barrientos et al., 2011). However, this may not universally be the case for all industrial clusters. For instance, in the case of mining clusters, one might imagine that the work to be performed inside these mines could still be described as low-skilled, labor-intensive work where the prospects for women's social upgrading may be more limited (Jenkins, 2014). Exploring the interaction between producer-driven value chains and local industrial clusters in relation to women's social upgrading or downgrading in such contexts may be particularly interesting in future studies.

NOTES

1. Social upgrading consists of two parts, first, measurable standards and second enabling rights (Barrientos, 2019b). Measurable standards involve those that can relatively easily be quantified such as the type of employment (whether regular or irregular), wages, work hours, overtime, and social protection levels (Barrientos and Smith, 2007). Enabling rights include the right to collective bargaining, freedom of association, non-discrimination, empowerment, and voice. Without these enabling rights it may be difficult for workers to negotiate with their employers in order to secure improvements in more measurable standards of work (Gereffi and Lee, 2016). *Social downgrading* refers to a situation in which workers experience job losses, declining wages, unpaid overtime, forced labor, and deterioration in the levels of social protection, implying the removal (or absence) of enabling rights (Pyke and Lund-Thomsen, 2016).

2. In the industrial cluster literature, the term "devil's deal" was first introduced by Tendler (2002) to describe a tacit agreement between politicians and small-firm owners by which these owners would vote for the politicians in local elections in exchange for (a) not collecting taxes from these firms; (b) not enforcing environmental or labor regulations; and (c) keeping police and government inspectors from harassing them. Here we use it in a new way in relation to the gendered nature of women's social upgrading and downgrading in industrial clusters.

3. These relate to "more advanced and differentiated mass producers which for the most part prospered in the import substitution period and mainly produce for the domestic market. They typically comprise a heterogeneous mix of enterprises ranging from petty producers to large Fordist industries. Trade liberalization forced these clusters to face international competition and induced far-reaching structural change" (Altenburg and Meyer-Stamer, 1999, p. 1695).

4. These are defined as clusters involving "technologically more complex activities, such as the electronics and auto industries. These clusters are dominated by large branch plants of world-class manufacturers and usually serve both national and international markets" (Altenburg and Meyer-Stamer, 1999, p. 1695).

5. Worker-centered perspectives

INTRODUCTION

At the outbreak of COVID-19 in the spring of 2020, millions of garment workers in Asia were faced with the prospect of either losing their jobs or risking a significant cut in their salaries and social benefits (Leitheiser et al., 2020). The outbreak of COVID-19 thus raised significant questions for not only workers and trade unions in terms of how they could meaningfully defend workers' conditions and rights in a context of value chain disruptions and a global economic recession setting in (Anner, 2020). It also implied that brand representatives and local factories had to face hard questions about what was dubbed "responsible supplier disengagement." In short, how should brands take "social responsibility" for workers that were affected by the global economic slowdown. Such issues included, for instance, whether, and if so to pay wages earned to workers, how to "responsibly" and legally lay off and rehire workers, ensuring that fired workers were compensated in accordance with national laws, received social insurance and pension payments for the time that they had been employed at garment export factories (SOMO, 2020). Such issues became even more pertinent in a context where some governments used the advent of COVID-19 to reduce worker protection and impose further restrictions on the freedom of association and right of workers to engage in collective bargaining (BBC News, 2020).

The debate about responsible supplier (dis)engagement can also be seen as an extension of the buyer-driven cooperation paradigm to CSR in GVCs. As mentioned in Chapter 2, this paradigm advocates the use of long-term trading relations between buyers and suppliers, revising buyer purchasing practices, capacity building of local supplier management and worker representatives in buyers' corporate codes of conduct, as well as participation in multi-stakeholder initiatives and the use of "local resources" such as NGOs and trade unions in year-round monitoring of work conditions at supplier factories (Lund-Thomsen and Lindgreen, 2020). More recently, brands, trade unions, international organizations, NGOs, donor agencies in the Global North, and multi-stakeholder initiatives have also advocated the use of so-called "social dialogue," or "all types of negotiation, consultation, or simply exchange of information, or among, representatives of governments, employers and workers" to resolve worker–management conflicts, and advance industrial as well as social peace (ILO, 2021). In short, the cooperative paradigm to CSR in GVCs, along with the more recent emphasis on social dialogue in GVCs, is partly intended to enhance the agency of workers to collectively defend their own work conditions and labor rights at the base of GVCs (Lund-Thomsen and Coe, 2015; Oka et al., 2020b).

In this chapter, I explore whether the cooperative approach to CSR in GVCs enables or constrains workers' ability to collectively organize and demand improvements in their work conditions in the context of a global economic slowdown. Obviously, COVID-19 is not the first global economic slowdown in recent times. It was preceded by the global financial crisis of 2008–2009. Hence, in the spirit of "looking backwards in order to rebuild better," I revisit an earlier experiment where a global brand, Nike, attempted to enhance the labor agency of workers through capacity-building measures advocated as part of the cooperative paradigm to CSR in GVCs. In other words, I try to answer the question: under what circumstances do the CSR initiatives of internationally branded companies facilitate or constrain workers' agency in export-oriented industries in developing countries?

The literature on labor agency in GVCs has usually conceived of labor agency as workers acting collectively through trade unions with the aim of defending their rights and improving their conditions of work (Cumbers et al., 2008; Riisgaard, 2009; Riisgaard and Hammer, 2011; Coe and Jordhus-Lier, 2011; Coe and Hess, 2013). As Riisgaard and Hammer (2011) point out, however, the ability to construct such "associational" power is ultimately driven as much by the local and national institutional context – often termed the "horizontal" dimension – as it is by transnational GVC structures – the "vertical" dimension. More recently, labor agency in GVCs has also been understood in terms of unorganized workers opting in and out of particular work forms and kinds of employment. In this literature, the focus has been on how the decision-making processes of workers in relation to their choice of work form/occupation have been facilitated or constrained by their embeddedness in local socio-economic contexts (Carswell and De Neve, 2013; Lund-Thomsen, 2013).

In this chapter, I contribute to this emerging literature on labor agency in GVCs (Kumar, 2019; Gansemans and D'Haese, 2019; Graz et al., 2020) by investigating the circumstances under which the CSR policies of internationally branded companies, in this case Nike, may facilitate or undermine worker agency at the level of supplier factories. Hence, this chapter explores how measures advocated via CSR (policy coordination between sourcing and CSR personnel, improved human resource management practices, training of workers, and year-round monitoring of work conditions at supplier sites) affect labor agency by using a case study from Pakistan.

In sum, this chapter seeks to make two distinct contributions to the embryonic literature on labor agency in GVCs. First, I seek to evaluate the potential of new modes of CSR transmitted through the "vertical" dimension of GVCs to facilitate worker agency in developing country suppliers, given wider cost and competitive pressures within a context of global economic crisis. Second, while granting worker rights may be an element of such CSR initiatives, I argue that their ultimate effectiveness is shaped by the activities of a variety of local and national actors in the production context. Both analytically and empirically, I map out the "horizontal" elements that co-determine the scope for worker agency in combination with wider GVC dynamics.

I use a pilot carried out by Nike in the football manufacturing industry of Pakistan in 2008/9 as my case study. In this case Nike attempted to coordinate its sourcing and CSR policies, improve human resource management practices by providing workers with productivity incentives, train workers in their rights under Pakistani labor law and the Nike code of conduct, and conduct year-round monitoring of work conditions at its supplier factory in Pakistan. My main line of argument is that Nike's pilot seems to have been undermined by the eruption of the global financial crisis in 2008 and actor politics in Nike's GVC that followed in the wake of the crisis. In fact, the crisis made it financially unviable for Nike's supplier factory to fully comply with Nike's new CSR approach in 2009. At the factory level, worker agency was not facilitated by the integration of Nike's sourcing and CSR policies, its added productivity incentives, or year-round monitoring of work conditions. However, training factory workers in their rights under Pakistani labor law and Nike's code of conduct appeared to raise their level of awareness to such an extent that they organized strikes and were partly successful in having their demands met.

The chapter is structured as follows. In the next section, I develop an analytical framework that conceptualizes the circumstances under which internationally branded companies facilitate and/or constrain workers' agency in export-oriented industries in developing countries through the use of the new approach to working with CSR in GVCs. I then briefly introduce the methodology that underpinned this study. The empirical analysis is subsequently divided into two sections. I first introduce the Sialkot cluster and Nike's role within it before exploring the impacts of CSR imperatives transmitted through the vertical dimension of the production networks on the potential for labor agency. Second, I explore the role of local and national Pakistan-based actors – constituting the horizontal dimension – arguing that the role of these actors is crucial in shaping worker agency and ultimately the effectiveness of Nike's recent interventions from the worker perspective. Finally, the conclusion outlines the main findings and the policy implications of the analysis.

ANALYTICAL FRAMEWORK: CONCEPTUALIZING LABOR AGENCY IN GVCS

My analytical framework seeks to explain how a multinational company's sourcing and CSR policies may facilitate and/or constrain labor agency at the level of local supplier factories in developing countries. In this chapter, my use of the GVC approach reflects my wish to explore how CSR and labor agency are embedded in wider networks of relationships. These include not only global lead firms and suppliers in developing countries, but also other actors such as international and national regulatory authorities, international NGOs, worker organizations, and the media. I see these wider networks as playing crucial roles in determining what is produced, where, when, in which quantity and at what price in GVCs. In addition, I am concerned with how the relationship between CSR and labor in GVCs is embedded in local socio-economic contexts. Hence, both formal (in the form of national laws and implementation agencies) and informal institutions (such as values, norms, and beliefs) are seen as important in structuring the way in which GVCs are governed. These factors also have to be taken into account when analyzing the gains or losses accruing to local firms, contractors, and workers from GVC restructuring, including the kind of restructuring that follows from the implementation of CSR policies in GVCs.

In the analytical framework I also draw a distinction between vertical and horizontal relations in the analysis of GVCs (Neilson and Pritchard, 2009, 2010). I follow Riisgaard and Hammer (2011) in arguing that labor agency within GVCs can only be understood in terms of the intersection of these two dimensions. They posit that "the governance of interfirm linkages, while crucial in structuring the terrain for labor, is always mediated by the specific social relations of local production and labor control regimes as well as the histories and orientations of the respective actors" (p. 183). They argue that the potential for worker agency is shaped by the intersection of three factors: the overall "drivenness" of the network, whether it is a producer- or buyer-driven system, and the nature of the local labor control regime.

The vertical dimension of GVC analysis thus has to do with the role that internationally branded firms play in determining the terms of GVC participation for local firms, contractors, and workers. If orders from international buyers are stable, and if buyers supply workers with a range of CSR benefits including bonus incentives, overtime payments, and social insurance, workers may be in a better position to bargain for higher wages and demand more benefits associated with their employment in a local supplier factory (Selwyn, 2008; Oxfam, 2010). However, the provision of CSR benefits does not automatically improve workers' bargaining position. As De Neve (2014) shows, the introduction of CSR policies might actually drive some categories of workers into the informal sector. De Neve describes how working 9–5 in strictly controlled CSR-compliant factories working at a high pace may – in some cases – result in workers losing the freedom to influence their work process and end up with them earning lower wages. Working in such CSR-compliant factories may also push some women workers out of the workforce as this type of factory-based work may not be possible to combine with taking care of their home duties and child-rearing. Moreover, as Ruwanpura (2012) shows, the impact of CSR policies (taken here as corporate codes of conduct) on labor conditions may be uneven. For example, whereas the "no child labor" clause tends to be strictly enforced at export-oriented factory sites, other aspects of corporate codes of conduct, such as providing a living wage and ensuring freedom of association for workers, are often not implemented.

At the same time, providing workers with a range of CSR benefits might be part of the strategies used by international brands to respond to the demands of labor which could – for a certain period – contribute to creating a more loyal and productive workforce. Hence, as Selwyn (2009) demonstrated in his analysis of fruiticulture exports in North-East Brazil, many exporting farms introduced a range of real benefits (e.g., subsidized housing and welfare benefits) for workers, with the aim of reducing their links to the relatively militant rural trade unions in the area. This reflects the concern in the CSR literature with securing a business case for CSR, through which companies maintain their profitability by incorporating social and environmental concerns into their core business operations (Blowfield and Frynas, 2005, Oka et al., 2020b).

Hence, if curbing labor agency is an intended outcome of brands and their suppliers introducing CSR schemes in GVCs, an unintended consequence of introducing a range of CSR benefits to workers at the bottom of GVCs may be to stimulate worker agency in instances where brands and suppliers fail to deliver on their CSR promises. For example, if buyers do not provide regular orders to their suppliers, this places local producers in a situation where they might not be able to run a financially profitable operation during those times when their order books are low (Ruwanpura and Wrigley, 2011). In turn, this might trigger the agency of workers as they realize that they are not provided with the promised CSR benefits.

GVCs also play an important role in determining the scope for labor agency to the extent that international buyers operate with stringent CSR requirements. In instances where these buyers demand strict compliance with such requirements, local manufacturers are likely to be under greater pressure to listen to the demands of the workers they employ (Riisgaard and Hammer, 2011). Conversely, if local manufacturers are serving international customers that are not concerned about CSR compliance, the scope for workers to have their voices and demands heard is likely to be more constrained. In such instances, workers may have little or no influence in terms of co-determining the conditions under which they labor (see also, Bair and Palpacuer, 2015).

The horizontal dimension, in turn, refers to the local socio-economic and community contexts in which developing country export industries are embedded (Neilson and Pritchard, 2010). In a study of aquaculture unionism in Chile, for example, Oseland et al. (2012) argue that worker agency in GVCs is heavily conditioned by national factors, with three domains being scaled heavily at the national level: the organization of labor networks, the regulation of economic and employment affairs, and the sphere of public discourse about work and its regulation. Similarly, as authors such as Brammer et al. (2012) and Gond et al. (2011) recognize, CSR is also interpreted and "translated" into national contexts where it is embedded in social networks, business associations, and political structures. It is within these national contexts that the sourcing and CSR policies of internationally branded buyers play a crucial role in facilitating or undermining labor agency at the "bottom" of GVCs. Accordingly, in the horizontal aspect of my analytical framework I identify four factors that are likely to mediate how the sourcing and CSR policies of internationally branded companies affect the scope for workers' agency in local supplier factories. These are the use of private-sector consultants, worker organizations, NGOs, and the presence/absence of an independent national media.

Second, trade unions have often been highlighted as a key vehicle for strengthening worker agency in GVCs. On the one hand, trade unions provide the means through which workers can articulate their joint interests and engage in collective bargaining vis-à-vis their employers. The rights to freedom of association and collective bargaining are therefore seen as critical in relation to improving workers' scope for influencing their employers. This is also known as "associational power" (Wright, 2000) which arises from the collective organization of workers in trade unions and political parties (Selwyn, 2008). On the other hand, trade unions in countries such as Bangladesh, India, and Sri Lanka have traditionally formed alliances with political parties. These parties have been involved in the formation of workers' organizations, while workers' organizations have tended to be incorporated within the broader decision-making structures of the state. This may circumscribe their ability to develop and support more "independent" transformative worker agendas that translate into real improvements in their work conditions in these countries (Candland, 2001; Gunawardana and Biyanwila, 2008; Miller, 2012).

At the same time, levels of unionization are often low in developing countries, potentially limiting their effectiveness as fora through which workers can jointly organize themselves. Trade unions in developing countries have also been criticized for being male dominated, sometimes corrupt and representing the interests of their leaders rather than the workers in whose name they speak. In these circumstances, their potential as a vehicle for articulating workers' demands may be quite limited. However, low levels of associational power do not necessarily translate into low levels of what Wright (2000, p. 962) describes as "structural power," that is, that which arises out of the strategic position of workers in the production system. Drawing on the work of Wright, Silver (2003) further subdivides structural power into two sub-categories: marketplace bargaining power and workplace bargaining power. The former arises in demand–supply relations, for example, in instances where there might be a shortage of skilled labor in particular industries which accordingly increases the bargaining power of workers. Workplace bargaining power has to do with the ability of workers to stop production flows which can have wider spill-over effects on employment relations (see also Selwyn, 2008). To this, I may add that labor agency is likely to be enhanced if workers labor in a central production site where they might be in a better position to organize themselves, and undermined if workers are situated in dispersed, subcontracted employment units, for example, small-scale workshops or home-based work.

However, labor unions are not the only fora through which workers may organize and defend their interests in factory settings. As the work of Wills (1999, 2000, 2001) has demonstrated, the existence of work councils could also potentially provide workers with a channel to communicate and articulate their concerns vis-à-vis management. Work councils exist in a variety of forms, particularly in Europe, but carry the promise of reducing workplace conflicts by systematizing and improving communication channels within factories and improving the bargaining power of workers through regular meetings involving workers (and sometimes company management). In theory, work councils could provide management with an opportunity to share the corporate vision, highlight the need for increasing productivity, and implement "best practice" in relation to shop-floor worker organization in a top-down fashion. For trade unionists (and other employees), such councils could be used to confront management with pressing worker concerns and discuss how improvements in work conditions might be obtained from the bottom-up.

Third, NGOs are also an important factor that may facilitate and/or constrain worker agency in GVCs. The involvement of NGOs in the governance of GVCs can also be seen as part of what Sunley (1999) calls stakeholder capitalism. Stakeholder capitalism embodies a commitment to finding "third way" solutions to economic and social problems that avoid the excesses of neo liberal market reforms and state-centered policymaking. In this context, the central idea of "stakeholding" not only implies that it may be financially profitable to include a broader range of actors in the management of company affairs (as opposed to the company only serving the interests of its shareholders). Stakeholding can also be seen as an ethical and moral imperative which – in the context of GVCs – involves company management, employees, retailers, consumers, producers, workers, and communities in more responsible forms of network governance (Hughes, 2001).

The question is, however, what happens when the abstract notion of stake-holding is operationalized in practice (Sunley, 1999) as, for example, when international retailers, suppliers, NGOs, and workers seek to jointly govern GVCs. On the one hand, the literature on public–private partnerships has emphasized that NGOs may help in terms of providing knowledge, resources, and context sensitivity to the work of corporations whose operations affect the livelihoods of local communities in developing countries. In particular, the ability of NGOs to interact with and organize communities in developing countries may provide an opportunity for corporations to improve their relations with local-level actors (Rein and Stott, 2009). In theory, NGOs might thus open a channel through which workers can communicate or articulate their demands in relation to their employers. On the other hand, as Hughes (2001) has shown in the case of ethical trading initiatives, stakeholding becomes very difficult to operationalize when actors with ideologically opposed viewpoints are asked to join hands in the formulation of criteria for responsible GVC governance. In fact, the literature on public–private partnerships also emphasizes the risk of NGOs getting "too close for comfort" when interacting with corporations. NGOs may lose their independence and legitimacy by working together with corporations as they adopt their values and ways of viewing the world (Baur and Schmitz, 2012). In this way, NGOs may become an actor that constrains the agency of workers in export-oriented industries in developing countries.

The final part of the framework deals with the role that local and international media may play in relation to facilitating and/or constraining worker agency in developing country export industries (cf. Oseland et al., 2012). On the one hand, if the local media is independent of government control in developing countries, news reports may play a key role in highlighting the plight of workers that are engaged in struggles with their employers over their work conditions. Bringing such struggles into the public realm may raise the stakes for their employers. Not only do they risk losing their public legitimacy, but also they might also face regulatory action from local authorities and/or losing their international customers if they do not heed their workers' concerns (Tran, 2011). On the other hand, if the local media is tightly controlled by government authorities, press freedom is non-existent, and critical journalists are persecuted, this is likely to constrain workers' ability to voice their concerns in the public realm. In this way, it may be difficult for workers to form alliances, either domestically or internationally, that might help them in bringing pressure on their employers to rectify their grievances. Hence, local media may be a critical factor in either facilitating and/or constraining worker agency in local supplier firms.

A NOTE ON METHODOLOGY

The chapter draws upon a wider comparative study of the work conditions in the football manufacturing industries of Pakistan, India, and China (Lund-Thomsen and Nadvi, 2010a; Khara and Lund-Thomsen, 2012; Lund-Thomsen et al., 2012; Lund-Thomsen, 2013). This study concentrated on mapping the GVCs linking international football brands, suppliers in the three countries, contractors and football stitchers engaged in factory, stitching center, and home-based work. A mapping process was also undertaken of the work conditions of football stitchers engaged in factory, stitching center, and home-based work across the production locations.

At the time of my fieldwork in late 2009, the Pakistani football manufacturing industry consisted of approximately 390 enterprises, many of which were small and medium-sized firms with 250 employees or less. Only a handful of companies could be considered large with 250 employees or more located at the factory site. The process of football stitching was outsourced to approximately 20,000 football stitchers at the beginning of my fieldwork when the financial crisis had affected the cluster the worst. This number increased to approximately 22,000 stitchers at the end of my fieldwork in November 2009. Out of these stitchers approximately 400–500 were working in Nike's main supplier factory, Silverstar, while the rest of the stitchers were laboring in village-based stitching centers in the supply chains of other international brands. These village-based stitching centers had been established to facilitate the process of child labor monitoring within the cluster. The centers would usually consist of a centrally located building or demarcated outdoor space which could either be rented by a contractor, owned by the factory or individual stitchers.

Interviews were undertaken with the sourcing and CSR personnel of leading international buyers from the Sialkot cluster including the international and local representatives of brands such as Nike, Adidas, UK-based Mitre, Danish Select Sports, and alternative brands such as Fairdeal Trading. These interviews focused on the history of the brands' involvement with the cluster, their perception of the competitive strengths and weaknesses of the cluster, their relationships with individual suppliers, their CSR requirements, and how they monitored the enforcement of these requirements. I then traced their supply chains to Sialkot, interviewing 11 local suppliers, including some suppliers in my sample that supplied footballs to non-branded international buyers in markets in the developing world. These interviews mostly focused on how their business was affected by their buyers' sourcing and CSR requirements, and how they monitored the presence/absence of child labor in their own stitching supply chains. I then took one further step down the supply network, interviewing eight contractors about how they carried out their work, supplying stitchers with panels and thread to stitch footballs and returning the stitched footballs to the factories in the center of Sialkot. Finally, I undertook – with the help of local research assistants fluent in Punjabi – 51 individual interviews and 11 focus group interviews with stitchers engaged in factory, center, and home-based football stitching. Individual interviews focused on football stitchers' basic conditions of work including issues such as salary payments, work hours, occupational health and safety, work intensity, and levels of social protection. The focus group interviews explored what football stitchers saw as the pros and cons of stitching footballs in factories, stitching centers, and/or home-based locations.

The evidence presented in this chapter draws primarily on interviews with Nike's CSR staff in the USA and via telephone, internal Nike policy documents, the CEO and CSR staff of its main supplier factory in Pakistan, Silverstar, the NGO Pakistan Institute of Labor Research and Education, Matrix Sourcing (a sourcing company working for Nike in Pakistan), Just Solutions (an international labor rights consultancy working for Nike), and 14 interviews as well as two focus groups that were carried out with male workers from Nike's main supplier factory, Silverstar, in 2008 and 2009. In addition to the issues identified above, the individual interviews with Silverstar stitchers also touched upon workers' level of awareness of Nike's CSR requirements, their perceptions of the consultants hired for CSR monitoring, their impression of the training sessions they attended regarding their rights under Pakistani labor law and Nike's code of conduct, as well as how they collectively organized themselves to have their demands heard from Silverstar's management.

NIKE'S FOOTBALL MANUFACTURING OPERATIONS IN SIALKOT: THE VERTICAL DIMENSION

This chapter is certainly not the first to focus on labor issues in the Pakistani football manufacturing industry. A substantial body of work has investigated the role of industry-led approaches to eradicating child labor in the Sialkot cluster (Hussein-Khaliq, 2004), multi-stakeholder initiatives aimed at combating child labor (Lund-Thomsen and Nadvi, 2010b, 2012), local manufacturer perceptions of Western CSR policies (Khan, A., 2007; Khan, F.R., 2007; Khan and Lund-Thomsen, 2011), work conditions in Nike's football supplier factories (Siegmann, 2008), the work conditions and labor agency of home-based women workers (Lund-Thomsen, 2013, Naz and Bögenhold, 2020), and the relationship between economic and social upgrading (Lund-Thomsen et al., 2012; Danish and Khattak, 2020). In another paper (Lund-Thomsen, 2013), I also argued that Nike's CSR policies systematically excluded female football stitchers from participation in Nike's GVC. In fact, Nike's CSR approach did not take into account how the local socio-economic context affected the participation of females in the football manufacturing workforce. In particular, Nike's CSR policies did not recognize how factors such as geographical distance, local patriarchal values in the stitcher community, modes of recruitment, and a diversity of livelihood strategies facilitated and/or constrained female stitchers' possibilities for engaging in factory-based work. In this chapter, I therefore concentrate on investigating how Nike's CSR policies affect labor agency amongst the male football stitchers employed at its main football supplier in Pakistan, Silverstar. My focus is on football stitching as this is the most labor-intensive aspect of the football manufacturing process.

Nike's involvement in the Sialkot football cluster can be traced back to the mid-1990s where the company began sourcing footballs from a supplier known as Saga Sports (Siegmann, 2008). The company's arrival in the cluster coincided with the emergence of international media reports that children were involved in football stitching in Sialkot's villages. As a result, an international multi-stakeholder initiative – the Atlanta Agreement – was formed, including internationally branded manufacturers, the International Labour Organization, the United Nations Fund for Children (UNICEF), Save the Children and the Sialkot Chamber of Commerce and Industry (Hussein-Khaliq, 2004). The Atlanta Agreement introduced a child labor monitoring mechanism in the cluster and several social projects aimed at transferring children from football stitching to school. Saga Sports played a key role in designing the Atlanta Agreement and initiated the switching of home-based stitching to the designated stitching centers described above (Khan, A., 2007). However, several years later, in late 2006, Nike announced that it would cut connections with Saga Sports due to labor rights violations occurring at the Saga Sports factory site and the unauthorized outsourcing of football stitching from centers to home-based locations. In early 2007, Nike re-entered the Sialkot cluster with a new supplier, Silverstar, introducing a new production and CSR model at the same time (Lund-Thomsen and Nadvi, 2010b).

Although the new production and CSR model included lean manufacturing principles, Nike's main requirements were that all workers had to be registered, full-time employees with aligned social benefits. Their pay should be based on an hourly wage with related performance bonuses. The new model also included worker and management training programs to educate workers on Nike's code of conduct/core labor standards, their legal rights under Pakistani law, and the importance of human resource management as the best way to maintain worker management dialogue and communication. Compliance with Nike's production and CSR requirements was to be closely monitored by Nike's agent in Pakistan – a sourcing company called Matrix Sourcing. CSR audits were also to be occasionally carried out by other third-party monitors. Training of workers was undertaken by the Pakistan

Institute of Labor Education and Research (PILER) – a well-reputed NGO based in Karachi – in cooperation with the UK-based labor rights consultancy company, Just Solutions. In this way, Nike's sourcing and CSR policies in relation to Silverstar sought to facilitate the agency of male factory-based workers in this factory.

At the time of my fieldwork in 2009, the male stitchers in Silverstar were all in their 20s or 30s, locals from Punjab province, engaged in full-time stitching 9 hours a day (8–5), and the main bread earners of their families. The monthly salary levels (PKR 7,540: PPP$ 263) and the working hours (9 hours a day) of the factory-based, Silverstar stitchers included in my sample tended to be slightly higher and longer than those of the center (PKR 5,460; PPP$ 191) and home-based stitchers (PKR 2,275; PPP$ 79) I interviewed. All of the stitchers were hired after mid-2007 when Silverstar began producing footballs for Nike. The workers had either completed primary or secondary education, allowing them to understand Nike's production and CSR requirements and were capable of keeping up with Nike's production requirements of having to stitch at least four match balls a day. The work was physically demanding, with each ball at times requiring more than 800 individual stitches. Sometimes the football stitchers would also suffer from work-related injuries such as needle pricks, deformed fingers, and backache from long hours of stitching in the same position (Lund-Thomsen, 2013). However, the value of their earnings (PPP$ 263 a month), while above the minimum wage and the highest offered in the industry, could hardly cover even the most basic amenities required to sustain a family. For example, an estimate of the NGO International Labor Rights Forum, indicated that a football stitcher heading a family of five would need PKR 12,000 (PPP$ 419) a month to sustain that family if food, education, electricity/gas, medical, housing and miscellaneous expenditures were to be covered (ILRF, 2010). Nevertheless, the Silverstar workers were supposed to be covered by social insurance (old age pension, medical insurance, and a one-off compensation in case they were laid-off).

In the analytical framework, I argued that vertical relations within the production network might be used as a driver for enhancing worker agency. Importantly, the ability of international brands to supply stable order volumes may facilitate the ability of workers to extract higher wages and fringe benefits from their employers. Conversely, if international brands could not provide regular orders to their suppliers in the developing world, this may have constrained the ability to negotiate with their employers for improvements in their work conditions. The latter process turned out to be the most important in my case study.

At the time of the research in 2009, the global financial crisis had recently erupted and was affecting the global football manufacturing industry. In practice, Nike was not able to place the order volumes that the factory owner had initially expected (around 300,000 footballs a month). Instead production levels were down to 60–70,000 balls in June/July 2009. As the volume of orders was low, the factory was not able to make any profits at the time. This placed considerable pressure on Silverstar's owner to reduce the factory's running costs. One way to reduce costs was by laying off 500–700 workers. According to the local sourcing company, Matrix Sourcing, workers were being paid the full gratuity that Silverstar was required to offer under Pakistan's labor laws. However, some of my individual worker and focus group interviews indicated that laid-off workers were not paid their compensation in full:

> Some people have been fired. Some have got their full payment, gratuity etc. Some are not paid in full. (Interview with Silverstar Worker)

The reduced amount of work also had other consequences for the implementation of Nike's production and CSR model in Silverstar. Some of the fringe benefits associated with stitching footballs were not paid in full either. This was the case with the stitchers' lunch money, for example, where football stitchers were supposed to be paid PKR 21 (PPP$ 0.73) daily that would allow them to buy their food at the Silverstar canteen.

> Then we used to get PKR 21 (PPP$ 0.73) for the meals but now they have reduced that amount to PKR 10 (PPP$ 0.35) … . They say our factory is in crisis situation so you wouldn't get the whole amount unless the factory's situation gets better. (Interview with Silverstar stitcher)

The financial crisis also affected Nike's production model in other ways. For example, workers who were stitching more than the required four balls a day were no longer receiving any bonus payments. One of the male Silverstar stitchers expressed how this happened:

> Around 30–40% of the people are facing this problem. These are the people who stitch five balls daily and every month they get PKR 500–1,000 (PPP$ 17.5–35) less salary somehow. When we go to them regarding their calculation, they ask us how many days have you worked for? This much. So they just complicate it and confuse us. The issue is that many people are not educated here so we are facing a lot of problems due to that. Whatever we are getting, we are thankful to Nike that apart from being the most renowned brand of the world, it asks for the quality work and also tries to give many facilities to workers. But unfortunately these facilities don't reach us. (Interview with Silverstar stitcher)

In summarizing this section on vertical relations, I can state that Nike's sourcing policy of reducing orders to Silverstar in mid-2009 had the effect of reducing workers' wages, fringe benefits, and gratuity payments. In other words, it appeared as if Nike's sourcing policy constrained the ability of Silverstar's male workers to extract higher wages and fringe benefits from their employer. This raises the question of the extent to which Nike' CSR policy might have facilitated the ability of Silverstar's workers to engage in labor agency within this wider macro-economic context. I explore this question in the next section, which investigates how Nike's sourcing and CSR policies interacted with the local context of work and employment in Sialkot – the horizontal dimension – in creating particular labor agency outcomes.

CONSTRAINED AGENCY? HORIZONTAL RELATIONS IN SIALKOT, PAKISTAN

In this section, I use the horizontal element of my analytical framework to explore how private-sector consultants, collective worker activities, NGOs, and national media in Pakistan facilitated and/or constrained labor agency at the Silverstar factory. I start out by looking at the role played by the private-sector consultants hired by Nike to monitor the implementation of its production and CSR requirements.

Private-Sector Consultants

My analytical framework highlighted that private-sector consultants might play a role in constraining labor agency in circumstances where they were paid to conduct rapid and superficial audits whose results remained unpublished. At the same time, this negative assessment saw such consultants as primarily being accountable to the multinational companies that hire them and not shop-floor workers. However, if private-sector consultants were to employ more participatory, worker-centered methods to auditing, these might embody the potential for serving as a channel for raising workers' concerns with their employers and end customers.

At the time of my fieldwork in Sialkot in mid-2009, a local sourcing company, Matrix Sourcing, was functioning as Nike's "eyes and ears" on the ground in Pakistan (and Sialkot, where Matrix had opened an office). However, the frequent presence of the Matrix production and CSR monitoring staff in the Silverstar factory did not appear to make any difference to the workers' ability to voice their concerns. As one male stitcher stated:

> ... we have this Matrix team ...they assured us in the beginning that if you have any problem, related to work, or related to your payments, you should come to us and complain. We go to them but they are not that helpful either, they just listen to us nicely but give no results.

The Silverstar football stitchers also mentioned that other CSR compliance monitoring teams (i.e., not Matrix Sourcing) would sometimes visit the factory. Usually, these consultants would spend time with the factory management of Silverstar before being taken on a tour of the factory accompanied by its management. They would rarely, if ever, directly attempt to speak to the workers. Hence, it appeared as if the visits of these monitors made little, if any, difference to the workers' ability to communicate their concerns related to their work conditions.

> Interviewer: What difference does it [the monitor's visit] make to your work conditions?
> Silverstar Stitcher: It does not make any difference to us. We work as a routine. They visit, they watch, and they leave.

In a similar way, some of the Silverstar stitchers indicated that the visits of these monitors might be helpful if the monitors were to speak directly to the workers. However, in practice, this did not happen and monitors tended to speak only to the Silverstar management as the two quotes from different workers illustrate below:

> They don't really let us access them. … No one has asked us whether we have any difficulties or trouble … they just visit briefly. They could, for example, ask the factory management to let them speak to a couple of workers. (Interview with Silverstar stitcher)
> I have seen that whenever the foreigners come for inspection, there are so many people of haji sahib [i.e., the owner] designated all around the team that no one dares to talk to them. If these problems could be communicated to them, workers would be in a better position. They will know then that the factory is taking all the facilities (i.e., lunch money, productivity incentives, annual bonus, and gratuity) from us but not passing it on to the workers. (Interview with Silverstar Stitcher)

In other words, it appears as if the CSR monitoring and audits conducted by private-sector consultants in the Silverstar factory did not facilitate the ability of Silverstar's workers to exercise labor agency in Nike's GVC. In fact, as described in the section on "vertical" relations, some of the male Silverstar workers praised Nike's for its progressive policies towards workers. However, as the workers had no direct line of communication with Nike, they could not formally voice their concerns to the US brand.

Work Councils

Another factor that might facilitate labor agency in Nike's GVC could be the existence of a local work council in Silverstar. As Wills (1999) pointed out, work councils can be a tool for management to communicate the company vision, emphasize the importance of increasing productivity, and introduce "best practices" for the organization of work in a topdown fashion. However, my analytical framework also emphasized that trade unionists might take advantage of their participation in work councils by impressing on the management the need to raise labor standards and improve work conditions from the bottom-up. Yet I also argued that worker agency can only ultimately be understood in relation to the local institutional and regulatory context.

In the case of Pakistan, the economic development path of the country paid virtually no attention to labor after Pakistan's independence from the British Empire in 1947 (Candland, 2001). To the extent that labor was allotted a role in this development, this was mainly as an industrial input that usually consisted of cheap labor from rural parts of the country. This labor extraction approach has since been institutionalized in various industrial relations and labor laws in post-independence Pakistan that place severe restrictions on the potential for progressive labor organizing (Candland, 2007). Hence, it may be difficult for Pakistani workers to exercise what Henderson et al. (2002) call "collective power." This refers to the actions that collective agents undertake with the aim of influencing the decision-making processes of firms, governments, and international agencies.

In my case study, the management of Silverstar was also against the idea of introducing a trade union in the factory. Instead the NGO PILER proposed to utilize the institution of "shop stewards" and the mechanism of a Joint Works Council under the Industrial Relations Ordinance 2002 (operative in 2008) which was accepted by the Silverstar management. Shop stewards were to act as a link between labor and management and to coordinate their interaction but did not have the right to engage in collective bargaining under the Industrial Relations Ordinance. The elections of shop stewards (two from each department) were held through secret balloting and the workers participated and elected about 25–27 shop stewards. These shop steward elections were organized by PILER and Just Solutions. My worker interviews indicated that the elections were held in a transparent way. As one of the male Silverstar stitchers put it:

> Interviewer: What do you say about that [elections being held]?
> Silverstar Stitcher: I think positively about that. Elections must be held. In every firm or factory the labor workers must have a representative ... they [the elections] were fair. The representatives were elected on the basis of votes. There was no issue with the elections. (Interview with Silverstar stitcher)

However, similar to the role that private consultants played in the factory, my worker interviews indicated that the presence of the elected shop stewards made little or no difference in relation to workers voicing their concerns vis-à-vis management or Nike for that matter. As another stitcher explained:

> Yes, there were elections and members were elected. But the members are poor and weak like us. When they are offered some money, they just become inactive and keep their mouths shut. Otherwise, we are well aware of how influential members can really be in an issue like this.

As the elected workers came from poor backgrounds, it appeared to be relatively easy for the management to dissuade them from taking any action. In fact, management pressure appeared to be an additional factor explaining why the shop stewards did not play any significant role in advocating workers' rights vis-à-vis the Silverstar management. One of the Silverstar stitchers explained:

> Because if these representatives speak in favor of the company, the owner of the factory is happy. And if these representatives talk in favor of the workers and labor, the owner of the factory is unhappy. What would they [the factory management] say? These people are not really good. These people create disturbance. This is what they do. They incite fellow workers. Right? They will say these things and as a result the factory owner will threaten these people.

Hence, it would appear as if neither Nike hiring private-sector consultants to monitor work conditions in Silverstar nor the election of shop stewards among Silverstar's stitchers had a positive impact on what Wright (2000) calls the associational power of workers. This raises the question of whether involving local NGOs in training workers in their rights under Pakistani labor law and Nike's code of conduct might be more successful in facilitating labor agency among Silverstar's stitchers.

NGOs

As argued in my analytical framework, local NGOs may facilitate labor agency at local supplier factories by bringing knowledge, resource, and context sensitivity to the work of corporations whose operations impact on workers and local communities in developing countries. This could occur, for example, through opening a channel of communication between the workers and their end customer, the internationally branded company. However, NGOs may also be co-opted into the worldviews of corporate managers, losing their critical approach and independence in instances where they come to rely on financial contributions from multinational companies to undertake their work. In this case, Nike's new CSR approach included a component that involved PILER providing training to Silverstar's workers about their rights under Pakistani labor law and Nike's code of conduct. Some Silverstar stitchers were quite critical of the training provided by PILER, indicating that the PILER staff and the Silverstar management appeared to be too close for comfort.

> The PILER people come here. We have meetings with them but they are just for the name sake. If we tell any problem in those meetings, 70% of the time, they take the owners side ... . Although they claim that we are here to tell you about your rights and how can you get those but on the other hand, if we raise our voice, they just speak the owner's language and don't listen to us.

However, while some workers indicated that they were skeptical of the PILER staff, most of my worker interviews indicated a very high level of awareness of the exact salary levels and fringe benefits that workers were supposed to obtain as part of their employment at the factory. Crucially, some workers indicated that they had achieved this awareness through PILER's training. Now they were able to calculate their exact wage and identify whether they had been paid the right amount or not. One of the workers explained how this worked in practice:

> You see this is my salary slip. The detail that appears here, you see. I stitched 87 footballs in about 20.5 working days. This is because they gave us leave during Fridays, Saturdays and Sundays due to shortage of work. We were scheduled to work for 18 days. So having worked for 18 days and completing this week 23 working days out of which I took leave for two days. This way I worked for 20.5 days, as one day I did not feel well and so I came home after 12 (and worked for half a day). They show here that they have paid me for that day. They show there that I have received PKR 6,760 (PPP\$ 236). [However,] this was not the amount I was paid.

While none of the Matrix Sourcing team, the shop stewards, and PILER appeared to be directly helpful in channeling the workers' demands vis-à-vis the Silverstar management, this increased level of awareness of their rights and responsibilities appeared to facilitate joint action among the workers. With all other communication channels blocked in the workers' perception, they began to organize spontaneous strikes when their wages and fringe benefits were either not paid in full or not paid on time. The leaders of these strikes turned out to be some of the more well-educated workers that were willing to stand up to the Silverstar management and were less afraid of losing their jobs.

In practice, these strikes would involve several workers. For example, in one instance, one of the workers explained how 70–80 workers had filed separate complaints about the manager that was in charge of salary calculations, some of them demanding that he be removed from this position. In another instance, some of the workers explained how they jointly engaged in a strike when they discovered that their salaries had not been calculated correctly.

> They had told us that they would pay us, as you know that they used to pay us PKR 21 (PPP$ 0.73) for roti (bread for lunch), but then they reduced it to PKR 10 (PPP$ 0.35) and at the same time they had told us that they would pay us PKR 5 (PPP$ 0.17) as extra bonus with each football.
>
> When the month ended on the 7th [July 2009], they did not pay anyone Rs. 5 bonus. So, the annual bonus of PKR 500 (PPP$ 17) was not paid. That means that they deducted the money from our wages but never paid it back. And the stitchers had expected it. Even though the stitchers are illiterate but they can calculate that they have stitched such and such number of footballs and so they must be paid the fitting amount.
>
> When they calculated with the number of footballs they had stitched they realized that they were not paid in full. So, they all gathered together and thus this strike continued till the 12th. They were told that they would be paid from the 12th day of the month. And the stitchers warned them that only if their wages would be from the 12th of the month, they would continue their work.

Several of the interviews conducted with the Silverstar stitchers indicated that these strikes were an effective way of having their demands met. As one of the workers stated:

> ... they only accept our demands when they are left with no choice. Had one or two persons approached then, you see the usual pattern is that if a couple of us approach them about something, as he [the owner] tells us that we should be at the most two people approaching him and discuss the matter with him ... . But if around 1000 workers gather together about a matter then he realizes how serious the matter is.

These events illustrate some of the inherent tensions in stakeholding. As Sunley (1999) describes, stakeholding embodies the potential for a more financially efficient, socially just and responsible form of company management. However, as Sunley also argues and as Hughes (2001) has demonstrated in the case of ethical trading initiatives, the politics of stakeholding involves bringing a very diverse set of actors together that tend to have conflicting goals and ideologies. Hence, in relation to GVC governance, stakeholding might not necessarily be more financially efficient as workers may decide to stop production when their demands are not met. However, as the Nike–Silverstar case shows, stakeholding may provide space for workers to influence their employers in such a way that more socially just solutions are found to industrial relations issues which might not have been possible without the buyer's (i.e., Nike's) commitment to stakeholding.

Hence, compared to the time when Nike's footballs were stitched in the decentralized stitching centers of Saga Sports in the villages around Sialkot, making it very difficult to organize workers, it appeared as if strikes were now a frequent phenomenon at the Silverstar factory. In other words, it seems that the centralization of football stitching and the training of workers in their rights and duties played a vital role in facilitating labor agency at the Silverstar factory.

National Media

The final part of my analytical framework pointed to the potential of national media in facilitating labor agency at the suppliers of internationally branded companies in developing countries. By highlighting the plight of workers in the public sphere, national media may pressurize local factories to respond positively to workers' demands. However, if freedom of the press is lacking, and journalists are persecuted by national authorities, this might act as a constraint on labor agency at the suppliers of internationally branded companies. The national media in Pakistan has traditionally been controlled by the ruling government, whether this was a civilian or a military government. However, President Musharraf, the former military ruler, decided to liberalize the media laws of Pakistan in 2004. This led to a mushrooming of private television channels out of which the GEO news channel is perhaps the most prominent. One of the workers explained how GEO had played an important role for the workers in terms of having their demands met during one of the strikes.

> There were about 250 to 300 employees protesting. Then someone phoned people from GEO (the media channel) as well. Actually the problem was not being resolved. Everyone was getting like PKR 1,000 (PPP$ 35), PKR 1,500 (PPP$ 52) or PKR 1,800 (PPP$ 63) as salary, but they issued only PKR 200 (PPP$ 7), PKR 250 (PPP$ 9) or at maximum around PKR 500 (PPP$ 17) or PKR 700 (PPS$ 24) to the same people. They kept everyone like that. Although, some people were given salary after 5 pm but it was too late. So, the workers went on strike the very next day. [The GEO people] phoned the owner of the factory and told him that they got a call from a worker and that they are coming to cover the news. The owner told them that the issue was resolved and there was no need for them to come now. (Interview with Silverstar Stitcher)

My interviews indicated that the issue was indeed solved. As another worker put it:

> Now you see recently there was a strike, the GEO [TV channel] representatives reached the factory gate. But they were held outside the gate and were not allowed inside. Meanwhile the strike had come to an end. By 12 o'clock they had accepted our demands and the strike had come to an end. (Interview with Silverstar Stitcher)

In other words, when workers were aware of their rights under national labor laws and a multinational company's code of conduct, and when they were able to gather together in a central production site, a free national media may enforce the structural power of workers or more specifically the workplace organizing power to stop production, as publicizing worker unrest through the national media may cause embarrassment for local factories and challenges in relation to their international buyers. This may have implications for the ways in which international brands, NGOs, and trade unions seek to empower workers in GVCs. This is an issue that I touch upon in the conclusion below.

CONCLUSION: CSR ALONE IS NOT ENOUGH

In this chapter, I set out to investigate the circumstances in which the CSR policies of internationally branded companies can facilitate or undermine workers' agency in export-oriented industries in developing countries. Using the case of Nike's production and CSR model in the Pakistani football manufacturing industry, my analysis demonstrated that most of the company's production and CSR requirements tended to have a limited impact on facilitating worker agency. In theory, Nike had attempted to coordinate its production and CSR policies by paying a premium price for the footballs it sourced, which would – at least partly – cover its suppliers' added costs of abiding with Nike's code of conduct. However, as Nike was not able to place the envisaged orders, its supplier factory, Silverstar, had to reduce its costs in order to stay afloat. This meant that many of the salary payments including added bonus incentives were not paid in full to the factory's football stitchers in 2009. This severely restrained the scope that workers had for reworking the system in ways that allowed them to extract extra benefits from their participation in Nike's GVC.

At the same time, Nike's use of private-sector consultants, the election of shop stewards, and training of workers in their rights under Pakistani labor law and Nike's code of conduct had differential outcomes. Nike's use of private-sector consultants appeared to block any possibilities of the workers directly communicating their concerns to Nike. The election of shop stewards had little effect on the ability of workers to collectively organize themselves and defend their rights vis-à-vis management. Most of these representatives were elected on the basis of friendship/kinship with workers from particular areas/villages in and around Sialkot. They tended to be quite weak and poor, and without the clout to challenge the management on non-compliance with Nike's code of conduct. However, the training of workers in their rights under Pakistani labor law and Nike's code of conduct appeared to raise the awareness of workers in such a way that they spontaneously began to organize strikes when their wages were not paid in full. And the publicizing of such strikes in local media had the potential to help facilitate labor agency in GVCs.

One could of course ask whether CSR would facilitate and/or hinder labor agency in same way during the early phases of COVID-19, as was observed during these events that happened more than a decade in Sialkot, Pakistan? On one hand, there is the parallel that the world was also faced with a global economic crisis in 2008/2009. However, the events of early 2020 differ since COVID-19 has been associated with both a global and economic slowdown and a simultaneous health crisis. In other words, these are two different types of crises, although they – at surface level – share certain similarities.

Anecdotal evidence suggests that the advent of COVID-19 might have had implications for work organization at the factory floor, related to social distancing measures and capacity building of management and workers in the use of hand sanitizers, facemasks, and frequent handwashing. COVID-19 has thus also been associated with increased health risks for workers, in particular for migrant workers that have sometimes had to live on-site in overcrowded hostels, where social distancing may not have been possible.

However, I would argue that the implications of the cooperative paradigm to CSR in GVCs for labor agency is best analyzed as a continuous process, rather than a fundamentally novel phenomenon that can be traced back to COVID-19. For instance, while workers in the Bangladesh garment industry have been exposed to increased occupational health and safety risks during COVID-19, they have also previously been exposed to health and safety risks, mainly due to lack of fire and building safety in the industry. This was powerfully illustrated in the Rana Plaza incident that killed almost 1,300 workers. For almost a decade now several initiatives have sought to remedy this situation by strictly monitoring and removing building and safety risks in the industry. In addition, anecdotal evidence suggests that capacity building of management and workers have sought to increase their awareness of these risks and how they can effectively be handled in a responsible fashion. Hence, whereas we lack detailed empirical studies of how the cooperative paradigm has affected labor agency in garment-producing countries during COVID-19, we may assume that some of the dynamics observed in the Nike–Sialkot case study could likely also be witnessed during the early phases of 2020.

This does not mean that we have not learned anything about the potential and limitations of the cooperative paradigm in enabling and/undermining labor agency in GVCs since the Sialkot case study was undertaken. On the one hand, more recent studies have confirmed the observation that national contexts of work and employment in labor-intensive export industries in the Global South place a constraining influence on labor agency. For instance, Gansemans and D'Haese (2019) identify issues such as weak employment protection, vulnerability of migrant workers, limited workers' representation, and insufficient labor law enforcement as constraints on labor agency in the pineapple plantation industry of Costa Rica.

However, there are also constraints on the ability of the cooperative CSR paradigm to enhance the agency of workers that are directly related to the so-called "business case for suppliers" for engaging in capacity-building initiatives. According to Oka et al. (2020b), factories are likely to save money by engaging in such capacity-building exercises, reduce workers turnover, and improve their productivity. Yet, empirical evidence suggests that capacity-building initiatives have not really scaled beyond a limited number of "best-in-class" suppliers. Moreover, return-on-investment calculations used by consultants and brands to convince suppliers to participate in these programs are often not transparent and simply not backed by sufficient evidence to convince suppliers of the business and worker benefits of these programs. In short, suppliers often do not make long-term changes in their worker management practices as a result of such initiatives, their implementation being both time-consuming and expensive for buyers and suppliers alike, and suppliers have difficulties in recovering costs and expanding their reach. As far as its effects on labor agency in GVCs, there is thus very little evidence to indicate that the cooperative paradigm enhances the agency of workers to actively negotiate and defend their rights in GVCs.

This leads me to revisit the theoretical framework that I set out at the beginning of this chapter. I highlighted the structural limitations that internationally branded companies face in relation to facilitating labor agency in export-oriented industries. As they are not directly responsible for managing the most intensive labor aspects of production, they not only outsource the financial risks associated with production to their suppliers, but also the labor management function which means that workers – instead of turning to Nike for proper payments of their wages – are left to bargain with a supplier firm that receives a relatively small share of the value added in the GVC for football manufacturing. However, to the extent that internationally branded companies may facilitate labor agency vis-à-vis their own suppliers, it appears that training workers in their rights is an important, initial step in incentivizing them to collectively organize and extract benefits from supplier firms in the GVCs of internationally branded companies. As such, the various kinds of place-based actors that constitute the horizontal dimension of GVCs become critical to facilitating worker agency. However, unless such training is supported by a conducive national context for worker organizing (which is clearly not the case in Pakistan), real doubts arise as to whether the Nike–Silverstar CSR model can be transferred to other buyer–supplier relations in the same or other industries. This is even more the case in instances where the buyer is not a giant multinational company which is concerned about its social or environmental reputation. Hence, national contexts for work and employment may place clear limits on what stakeholding can achieve in terms of facilitating more responsible forms of GVC governance. More broadly, progressive CSR initiatives within the vertical dimension of GVCs may, it seems, be a necessary but not sufficient factor for facilitating worker agency.

My analysis has also pointed to the real-world limitations associated with stakeholding at a time of global financial crisis. While stakeholding embodies the idea that it may be financially profitable to involve various actors in GVC governance, my case study shows that it may not be financially viable for suppliers to engage in CSR in the short term when order levels drop significantly. Clearly, compliance with CSR requirements remains a pre-condition for suppliers to enter the GVC of a company such as Nike. However, during periods of global financial crisis, the activation of labor agency may actually be intensified as the material benefits provided through CSR policies to some workers are temporarily not forthcoming.

6. Conclusion: corporate social responsibility in global value chains towards 2030

INTRODUCTION

In the final chapter of this book, I first recap the main research questions that I set out to answer in this book. I then outline its main line of argument, as I seek to provide answers to these questions. This leads me to outline future research implications for CSR in GVCs as we move towards 2030. Key topics identified here include: (i) CSR and the role of governments; (ii) CSR and human rights; (iii) CSR and climate change; and (iv) CSR and circular economy in GVCs. Finally, the chapter suggests various policy implications of the analysis undertaken in this book for different categories of stakeholders: (v) retailers and brands; (vi) suppliers; and (vii) workers, labor unions, and governments in the Global South.

THE MAIN ARGUMENT OF THIS BOOK

In the introductory chapter of the book, I set out to answer the following research question: *In which circumstances is it possible to identify a sweet spot in CSR in GVCs where the interests of buyers, suppliers, and workers in GVCs intersect?*

I subsequently added three sub-questions that I intended to explore in this book:

a. What are the drivers, main features, conceptual underpinnings, and limitations of the buyer-driven compliance and cooperation paradigms to CSR in GVCs?
b. Why are suppliers in the Global South that are integrated into GVCs often highly skeptical of CSR?
c. In which circumstances may the CSR policies of internationally branded companies facilitate or undermine worker agency at the level of supplier factories?

In this book, I suggested that we need to rethink CSR in GVCs, and that the dramatic events of COVID-19 as it erupted in early 2020 provided a useful entry point for such a reassessment of CSR in GVCs. My starting point was that there has been a tendency to discuss CSR in these chains from the vantage point of scholars and practitioners that – while based in the Global North – seem to sometimes overlook important perspectives and insights that emerge from detailed, in-depth, on-the-ground analysis of CSR as it unfolds in Global South contexts. In the world of CSR practice, this has often been combined with a tendency of global brand representatives, multi-stakeholder staff, consultants, and other "sustainability"/CSR specialists to ignore important concerns, interests, and voices of value chain participants such as suppliers, farmers, and workers in these Global South contexts. In order to address some of these shortcomings in current CSR theorizing and practice, I suggested that we could usefully rethink CSR in GVCs in a number of ways.

First, in terms of how we define CSR in these chains, I argued that it is important that we understand the contextual nature of CSR. In other words, how CSR is understood and framed will likely depend upon the societal contexts in which GVCs touch down. In other words, even if brands, retailers, and multi-stakeholder initiatives may claim to work with a "global" understanding of CSR, their understanding may not necessarily match those of suppliers, governments, NGOs, and trade unions in diverse national, institutional contexts within the Global South. My second key argument was that we need to unpack the contested nature of CSR in GVCs. We cannot assume that different stakeholders such as buyers, suppliers, and workers will necessarily have the same understanding of what constitutes "social responsibility": Instead they will likely have different interests, bargaining power, economic returns, and divergent norms/values in their practice of CSR. This needs to be factored into CSR theorizing and practice in the context of GVCs.

Third, I suggested that CSR needs to be seen as a dynamic concept that evolves over time. Hence, not only do GVCs evolve over time, our understanding of what constitutes social responsibility in these chains also evolves and within specific socio-economic contexts. In other words, simply because I have analyzed the relationship between CSR and labor agency in the Pakistani football manufacturing industry in the late 2000s, the same type of analysis might yield quite different results if I were to undertake the same analysis ten years later. In other words, Nike has most likely evolved in its CSR approach since then, the GVC for football manufacturing will have changed significantly in the last decade, the labor laws and regulations in Pakistan will no longer be exactly the same, and the nature of (constrained) labor agency in the industry will also have been altered.

With these key considerations in mind, I suggested that a useful approach to rethink CSR in GVCs is to undertake a critical appraisal of the so-called sweet spot in CSR in GVCs at which the interests of buyers, suppliers, and workers intersect to provide commercial benefits for buyers and suppliers in addition to improvements in the conditions of workers in GVCs. In turn, I then outlined the perspectives of these three central actors: namely, buyer, supplier, and worker perspectives on CSR in GVCs. Using these perspectives as a theoretical lens to understand CSR in GVCs, I theorized the circumstances under which the so-called sweet spot might emerge. I concluded the chapter by noting that – even if the prospects for finding such a sweet spot seemed quite limited – the chances would likely improve if trading relations between buyers and first-tier suppliers moved from market-based transaction towards hierarchical governance (using Gereffi et al.'s 2005 terminology).

Within this theoretical framing of CSR in GVCs, I suggested that there might be a need to rethink the two dominant buyer-centric paradigms on CSR in GVCs– the compliance and the cooperation paradigms – in the light of the eruption of COVID-19 in early 2020. My analysis demonstrated that events in the global clothing value chain during the early phases of COVID-19 made it relevant to expand our conceptual understanding of the compliance paradigm. However, the same events, as publicly reported through international media, did not lead to a need for fundamentally rethinking the cooperation-based approach to CSR in GVCs. In fact, the partial failure of buyers to act responsibly in relation to their purchasing practices and restrictions on international travel in early 2020 seem to have highlighted some of the already known limitations of the cooperation-based paradigm. In other words, many buyers still use "cut-and-run" policies, continue to pressure prizes in a downwards direction, and are not committed to long-term trading relations with their suppliers.

Rethinking CSR in GVCs along the lines of the contextually embedded, dynamic, and contested nature of this concept was also a key inspiration for my writing Chapter 3. Here I set out to answer the question: why are suppliers in the Global South that are integrated into GVCs often highly skeptical of CSR? To achieve this aim, I undertook a review of some dominant CSR conceptions that have been prominent in the last 20 years and developed a consolidated supplier-centered perspective on CSR in GVCs. I thus further unpacked a central theme in this book. Namely, that CSR definitions tend to be framed and promoted by key actors in the Global North, such that unique challenges and broader circumstances faced by suppliers and countries in the Global South are generally overlooked. I concluded that this also appears to be a central reason why many suppliers in the Global South are critical of CSR (as least as defined by global brands and other actors in the Global North).

In Chapter 4, I moved onto exploring whether a more "Southern-centric" supplier approach to understanding CSR in GVCs could be identified. I argued that supplier perspectives on CSR in GVCs should not only be understood as "individual supplier" perspectives. In fact, I highlighted that collective supplier approaches to engaging in CSR in GVCs may be equally important, in particular with reference to local industrial clusters in the Global South. By way of example, I asked how industrial cluster dynamics and approaches to CSR could contribute to the social upgrading of women workers that are inserted into GVCs? First, I highlighted that the cluster literature has not yet sufficiently explored the gendered nature of social upgrading within local economic districts that are tied into GVCs. Moreover, I underlined that local cluster insertion in GVCs was likely to lead to a re-articulation of pre-existing gender inequalities in ways that benefitted the functioning of GVCs but marginalized women workers. In this way, a devil's deal may exist regarding women's social downgrading in industrial clusters. While local cluster insertion in GVCs may facilitate local economic growth processes, this likely results simultaneously in social downgrading of women workers in the same local regions. I concluded that collective CSR interventions undertaken by suppliers are unlikely to fundamentally change these structurally embedded inequalities resulting from the interaction between cluster and GVC dynamics.

Finally, my concern with rethinking CSR along the lines of its contextually embedded, dynamic, and contested nature was also an inspiration for my writing the last chapter of the book. Here I sought to distill a so-called worker perspective on CSR in GVCs. In fact, I explored the circumstances under which CSR initiatives might facilitate and/or constrain labor agency in GVCs. I used a case study of Nike's sourcing and CSR policies in the football manufacturing industry of Sialkot, Pakistan to examine this question. This connected with a focus on how the afore-mentioned cooperation-based paradigm on CSR in GVCs enabled and/or undermined the agency of workers in this industry. My analysis demonstrated that CSR policies could create enhanced space for labor agency. However, that potential agency can also be thwarted by (i) wider economic forces within the global economy and (ii) relationships with local/national actors and regulatory frameworks. Hence, in understanding the potential and limitations for labor agency in GVCs, it becomes critical to analyze the intersection of these dimensions.

TOWARDS 2030: FUTURE RESEARCH AGENDAS ON CSR IN GLOBAL VALUE CHAINS

Having outlined the main arguments of this book above, I now consider what may become some of the dominant research themes in CSR and GVC research in the next decade leading up to 2030. In other words, what are the areas in which we fundamentally lack theoretical, empirical, and policy-oriented knowledge about CSR in GVCs? While these suggested areas for future research on CSR in GVCs are by no means exhaustive, I believe that there is a need to further explore (a) the role of governments in CSR in GVCs; (b) the relationship between human rights, CSR, and GVCs; (c) CSR, GVCs, and climate change; and (d) circular economy, value chains, and CSR.

Governments, CSR, and Value Chains

The role of governments in CSR in GVCs is still an underexplored topic. In the context of the wider argument in this book, finding the sweet spot in which the interests of buyers, suppliers, and workers intersect may not be possible without the active participation of national governments. Some may even rightly argue that it may be naïve to even think or suggest that finding such a sweet spot may be possible without considering the role of governments. Indeed, as authors in the regulatory renaissance tradition have demonstrated in the case of Brazil before the time of the current government, health and safety has improved, labor standards been enforced and workers been able to access labor rights, while greater mechanization was introduced in response to labor regulation. This proved to be a counter-balance to the neoliberal discourse on the retreat of the state, but also affect industrial strategy (Coslovsky, 2014; Nadvi, 2014).

This serves as a reminder of just how understudied and undertheorized the role of the state is in the regulation of CSR in GVCs that touch down in producer countries. Yet, as argued by Pyke and Lund-Thomsen (2016), social upgrading in industrial clusters, including those that are tied into GVCs, are influenced by state monetary, fiscal, and labor policies and regulations, as well as by dynamic processes of agency among cluster governance actors. Hence, Frank Pyke and I argued that the state's policies and regulations might enable or constrain cluster actors to behave in ways that affect social upgrading or downgrading. As such, we suggested that the state could both directly change social conditions in cluster contexts, promote social upgrading, with the aim of enhancing the government's overall economic strategy. Research in other contexts have demonstrated that the role of the state in enhancing social upgrading in the Global South is sometimes mixed. Some authors have suggested that some producer governments articulate the case for lower standards and wages in their countries in order to promote their competitiveness (Candland, 2001, 2007). It may also be that some developing country governments do not welcome CSR initiatives in GVCs. In the case of the Bangladesh Accord, it appeared that the Bangladesh government was hesitant to extend its mandate beyond the initial functioning of this multi-stakeholder initiative. In part, because the government felt that it had no voice or influence in the initiative (see for instance, Leitheiser et al., 2020).

This points to the need for further theorizing the role of the state in CSR in GVCs. On the one hand, a useful starting point may be Horner's (2017) categorization of the role of the state in GVCs as referring to the state as (i) a regulator, (ii) a producer (through state-owned enterprises), and (iii) a buyer (through public procurement). This would point towards a research focus on the role of the state in not only regulating labor and environmental standards of export-oriented enterprises in producer countries; it would also indicate a research focus on how the state – through government-owned enterprises – may play an important role in the implementation and enforcement of CSR guidelines and regulations. Moreover, the state could (and maybe de facto in some countries) play a vital role in demanding compliance with particular CSR criteria for local and international firms through its procurement policies. This could also be related to other changes in the global political economy where some states are moving towards exerting more nationalist economic tendencies, thus increasing their influence of value chains that touch down within their national boundaries. Hence, paying more detailed attention to the multi-faceted role of the state in regulating, enabling, and participating in global, regional, and national value chains will be a worthwhile research effort as we move towards 2030.

In this context, it may also be increasingly important to look at the interaction between public authorities and private-sector actors in the regulation of CSR in GVCs. For instance, in the context of their analysis of regional apparel value chains in Eswatini and South Africa, Pasquali et al. (2020) underline the critical role of public governance in influencing retailers' and suppliers' participation in RVCs in different ways. First, public governance is exerted through regional "trade regimes" that protect regional exporters from global competitors, and shifts in global trade regimes. Second, public governance is influential through national and regional "investment regimes" that facilitate investment flows from South Africa to Lesotho and Eswatini. This also includes the recent shift of US-oriented suppliers towards regional markets. Finally, "labor regimes," such as lowering wages, having less comprehensive labor legislation, and weaker trade unions in Lesotho and Eswatini compared to South Africa are important to the functioning of regional value chains.

However, as pointed out by Cashore et al. (2021), it may be helpful to move beyond a simple conceptualization of public policy and private authority as either competitive or complementary. As the authors argue, and I contend that this would also be helpful in conceptualizing and empirically analyzing CSR in GVCs, there is a need for mapping a fuller suite of mechanisms through which public and private governance interact. For instance, Cashore et al. argue that there are sub-categories of interaction which are not adequately dealt with in current CSR scholarship. These authors thus make a distinction between collaboration, coordination, and isomorphism as part of complementary interaction between public and private authority (in this book: this obviously relates to CSR in GVCs). In the competitive category, they refer to substitution and cooperation as important terms. In addition, they introduce the interesting term, co-existence, which represents a middle ground between these two extremes, consisting of both layered institutions and the possibility of chaos.

Hence, while they all have different and divergent starting points, the works of Horner (2017), Pasquali et al. (2020) and Cashore et al. (2021) all point to the need for a more nuanced theoretical and empirical understanding of CSR in GVCs. In fact, there seems to be a lot of potential from both drawing insights from the GVC and CSR literatures to understand the role of the state in relation to CSR in GVCs. This also relates to understanding the state as a dynamic and agentic actor whose role in CSR in GVCs changes over time across different institutional contexts (Moon and Knudsen, 2021).

Global Value Chains, CSR, and Human Rights

Another research area worthy of attention in the period leading up to 2030 is the increased emphasis on human rights and environmental due diligence in GVCs. Recently, the OECD adopted its Due Diligence Guidelines for Responsible Business Conduct. The guidelines are intended to help businesses to avoid and address adverse impacts related to "workers, human rights, the environment, bribery, consumers and corporate governance that may be associated with their operations, supply chains and other business relationships" (OECD, 2018, p. 3). The guidelines recommend that businesses should: (a) embed responsible business conduct within organizational policies and management systems; (b) identify and assess adverse impacts in operations, supply chains, and business operations; (c) cease, prevent, or mitigate adverse impacts; (d) track implementation and results; (e) communicate how impacts are assessed; and (f) provide for or cooperate in remediation when appropriate (OECD, 2018, p. 21).

The emphasis on due diligence is mirrored in several legislative initiatives that seek to hold companies to account for their human rights and environmental impacts in GVCs. These include the 2017 "Duty of Vigilance Law" of France which requires all large French companies – with over 5.000 employees – to undertake due diligence with regards to companies they control and all their contractors and suppliers (Schilling-Vacaflor, 2021). Similarly, in 2019, the Dutch government instituted the Child Labor Due Diligence Act that obliges companies to assess whether their goods or services have been produced with the use of child labor. In addition, Dutch companies are also supposed to develop a plan for preventing child labor in their supply chains (Van Kalmthout et al., 2021). In Germany, a draft supply chain act regulates due diligence obligations with respect to internationally recognized human rights. In its draft form, this piece of legislation will apply to partnerships and corporations that are headquartered in Germany and have more than 3,000 employees (Sharma and Kaps, 2021). At the level of the European Union itself, both the European Parliament and the European Commission have strongly advocated the enactment of legislation that will make human rights and environmental due diligence mandatory for companies in the European Union. In fact, the European Parliament's (2021) "Draft Directive on Corporate Due Diligence and Corporate Accountability" proposes legislation that will require companies to monitor, identify, prevent, and remedy human rights, environment and governance risks in their operations and business relationships, including suppliers and subcontracts (Sharma and Kaps, 2021). At the time of my finishing this book (May 2021), the European Commission has yet to propose legislation that makes similar requirements for human rights and environmental due diligence in the GVCs of European-based companies.

This new legislative development raises several interrelated questions. First, governments, suppliers, subcontractors, and workers from the Global South appear not to have had any significant involvement in the elaboration of these new European legislative initiatives. This is in spite of the fact that they are likely to be affected by these new measures. Perhaps unsurprisingly, this seems to reinforce an existing trend towards excluding value chain actors from the Global South in the formulation and execution of top-down CSR initiatives in GVCs (see for instance, Khan and Lund-Thomsen, 2011; Cheyns, 2014; Van der Ven et al., 2021).

Another drawback in relation to the enactment of these new legislative measures is that they do not directly address the root causes of labor and human rights violations at the base of GVCs. These relate to the purchasing practices of global brands and retailers that are well known as drivers of low wages, excessive overtime, and unstable jobs/incomes for workers in the Global South (Khan et al., 2020). This is not a new insight in the debate on CSR in GVCs, but one that seems to be too easily forgotten amongst European policymakers. As early as 2006/7, the ETI impact assessment study identified purchasing practices as linked to the creation of poor working conditions in the Global South (Barrientos and Smith, 2007).

For suppliers in the Global South, the increased costs associated with data gathering, reporting, and management in the Global South are likely to further increase production costs without bringing any immediate financial benefits to suppliers. This can thus be seen as what Ponte (2019) calls a supplier squeeze where sustainability management becomes another cost and pre-condition for the participation of suppliers in GVCs. There will be a need for hiring more sustainability employees and consultants in the years to come. This will likely further result in more reports, paper trails, factory inspections, and time spent on producing, managing, and storing information about human rights impacts at the level of suppliers and their subcontractors. This comes at a time when many suppliers have been suffering from audit fatigue – that is, very frequent and uncoordinated audits demanded by brands and retailers, who most frequently insist that suppliers must cover the costs of third-party audits (Khalid et al., 2020). In a recent article, Lund-Thomsen et al. (2021) document how retailer and multi-stakeholder sustainability documentation requirements take away important time for regulatory intermediaries in the cotton value chains of Pakistan and India that seek to build the capacity of local farmers to comply with the sustainability of the Better Cotton Initiative.

Another downside associated with the enactment of these new types of legislation is that they will favor large enterprises, not only among European importers but also large suppliers in exporting countries that have the (wo)man power, time, and resources to engage in extensive data gathering exercises. Medium-sized and smaller-scale suppliers may not have the time, financial resources, or specialized skills required for complying with these new human rights and environmental due diligence documentation requirements. Hence, the paper work associated with these new legislative measures may become a technical barrier to trade for small-scale suppliers, leading to their exclusion from GVC participation and subsequent negative consequences for local employment in the Global South. In fact, medium and small-scale enterprises are often amongst those that are providing most jobs to relatively poorer (and sometimes marginalized) groups (Jamali et al., 2017), but they are also the ones that typically face the largest challenges in complying with sustainability standards (Sommer, 2017).

It could also be argued that the new legislation being advocated by many human rights, consumer, and labor rights organizations in the European Union may be a thinly veiled attempt at intervening into the domestic regulatory affairs of large exporting countries in the Global South such as India, China, and Brazil by applying extra-judicial measures. In other words, to ensure the extra-territorial application of European Union legislation in relation to business entities that conduct trade relations with companies in countries that are not part of the European Union. In short, European governments are enacting legislation that affect suppliers in the Global South without either the suppliers or their governments having had any voice in the formulation of the same initiatives.

There may also be another unintended consequence of the introduction of EU legislation on mandatory human rights due diligence. In recent years, some governments in the Global South have tightened legislation around foreign support to civil society organizations, making it more difficult for these to operate. For instance, in India, the FCRA law has recently been amended to further complicate financial transfers between entities outside of India and organizations operating inside the country. It would appear that the tightening of legislation is partly related to the Indian government's view that the work of these organizations constitutes a hindrance to national economic development. In addition, it would also appear that the Indian government sees the work of some of these organizations as contrary to the national interest (Jalali, 2008). Finally, the Indian government may be sensitive to negative foreign press about issues which the government considers to be of domestic importance. So in short, the introduction of this foreign legislation may be seen as a further intrusion into domestic Indian affairs (Thrandardottir and Mitra, 2019). Whereas India officially gained independence from the United Kingdom in 1947, the adoption of this new legislation may in all likelihood be deemed as another post-colonialist attempt at reinforcing unequal and dependent trade relations between Europe and the subcontinent.

Just to be clear. I am *not* arguing that I oppose the enactment and implementation of human rights legislation both inside and outside of the EU. In fact, observance of human rights in both European importer countries and also producer countries in the Global South should be de facto observed. However, I am questioning the wisdom of not including value chain actors and governments in the Global South in discussions about EU legislation that produce widespread effects in these countries.

Global Climate Change, CSR, and Global Value Chains

Critics might rightly argue that this book has largely focused on labor issues in GVCs at the expense of a more environmentally oriented focus. In fact, most of the literature on CSR in GVCs has zoomed in mainly on labor issues in these chains (Lund-Thomsen and Lindgreen, 2014, 2020), whereas there has been a move in the wider CSR literature to employ the term, "corporate sustainability," reflecting a (re)newed focus on environmental issues in relation to the wider societal responsibilities of business (Montiel, 2008; Bansal and Song, 2017). However, this use of the term "corporate sustainability" has not yet been systematically discussed and employed in the GVC literature. Hence, the continued emphasis on social and labor issues in "CSR" in GVCs would seem to privilege an anthropocentric view of the world at a time when the global climate change crisis is placing our planet in peril.

In other words, there is a significant need for unpacking environmental issues more substantially in GVC research, particularly as environmental issues are now taking center stage for many global lead firms (Riisgaard et al., 2020). Unlike our colleagues in supply chain research, the GVC community of scholars is still lagging behind in our understanding of the environmental underpinnings, limits to, and impact of the functioning of GVCs. This is not to say that attempts have not been made at bringing "the environment" into GVC analysis (Bolwig et al., 2010; Riisgaard et al., 2010). For instance, Campling and Havice (2019) note that there is a small and growing literature that seeks to bridge GVC analysis and "the environment." They note that this embryonic literature embraces the following thematic areas: (i) the materiality of value chains; (ii) environmental upgrading; (iii) waste and post-consumption; and (iv) culture and ecology in networks of global production. What is remarkable about this categorization of the GVCs and environment literature is the lack of detailed theorization and empirical studies on GVCs and climate change in their own right.

Perhaps the closest we can come to studies that conceptualize and empirically bridge GVC and climate change analysis is the work of Ponte (2019, 2020) and Böhm et al. (2015). Ponte argues that "green capital accumulation" is related to how lead firms (typically retailers and supermarkets) GVCs address sustainability issues as a source of value creation and capture. Thus, Ponte highlights that sustainability management is emerging as a fourth capitalistic dynamic in addition to cost minimization, flexibility, and speed in GVCs (Coe and Yeung, 2015b). The work of Ponte, de Marchi, and other scholars also pointed to the potential and limitations of "environmental upgrading" of suppliers in Global South contexts where the profits of these suppliers are increasingly squeezed (Khan et al., 2020). Furthermore, Böhm et al. (2015) have analyzed how global carbon markets provide opportunities for profit, marketing, and legitimacy to companies whose value chains span the Global North and South. Their empirical work (in relation to a global energy company's investment in a Clean Development Mechanism project in India) highlights the discrepancies and tensions between corporate green commitments and economic, social, and environmental realities "on the ground." In addition, the work of Krishnan (2018) points to a need for further conceptualizing and empirically investigating the links between economic, social, and environmental upgrading in GVCs (Krauss and Krishnan, 2016).

In addition to these advancements in the environmental aspects of "CSR in GVCs" research, I would propose that there is an increasing need for bridging GVC and climate change research. I here share with Ponte (2019, 2020) and Böhm et al. (2015) a desire to understand sustainability management as part of the competitive dynamics of global lead firms in value chains. However, the GVC literature lacks strategic insights into the drivers, processes, opportunities/barriers, and consequences of climate change for the global organization of economic activity in value chains, and their implications for economic, social, and environmental upgrading in the Global South. Hence, I believe that future research on GVCs and climate change should address this gap. Specifically, there is a need for going beyond the above-mentioned studies by bridging GVC and climate change analysis in four significant ways:

i.   conceptualizing and empirically investigating the actors that drive climate change mitigation and adaptation within two interrelated industries: garment and textiles;

ii.   theorizing and gathering new empirical insights into the drivers, processes, opportunities, and barriers for climate change mitigation and
adaptation in the garments and textile industries; and

iii.   this type of combined GVC and climate analysis to an investigation of
its consequences for economic, social, and environmental upgrading
in garments/textiles industries of South Asia. In fact, it is worthwhile
investigating the interlinkages, trade-offs, and/or synergies that may
exist between labor rights and labor agency on the one hand and environmental concerns on the other hand. In addition, I would argue that

iv.   (i), (ii) and (iii) could be reached by linking multiple scales of analysis
(from the international to regional, national, and local) to a dynamic
perspective on GVC reconfiguration – i.e., during and (hopefully) after
COVID-19.

This leads me to explore another topic relevant to furthering a research agenda
that not only emphasizes the social/labor aspects of CSR but also dives into its
environmental dimensions: namely, CSR, circularity, and GVCs.

Circular Economy, Value Chains, and CSR

Another area in value chain research that is worthy of further attention in
the next decade is circularity. A number of international developments have
placed this issue prominently on the international agenda. First, the enactment
of the Paris Agreement and its goals for reducing CO_2 emissions has placed
international brands under pressure for reducing their CO_2 footprints in their
value chains (McKinsey & Co/GFA, 2020). Second, the overconsumption of
clothes associated with the fast fashion model, and its "quick use–throw away"
culture, has highlighted the lack of sustainability in current production and
consumption models in the global garments and textile industries (Anguelov,
2015). Third, pressure is increasingly emerging from institutional investors
that are increasingly concerned about the social and environmental footprint
of their investments, as well as climate-related risks, in addition to their traditional focus on financial returns (Krueger et al., 2020). Global brands are thus
under pressure to increase the transparency of their value chains, provide more
information about the environmental, social, and governance (ESG) aspects of
their operations, and demonstrate commitment to more sustainable production
models (Patil et al., 2020).

Moreover, new legislation from the European Union is compelling brands,
headquartered in Europe, to find more lasting solutions to the disposal of
garments and textiles waste. By 2025, EU policies oblige member states to
ensure that textiles are collected separately and that textile waste collected is
not incinerated or landfilled (EEA, 2019). There is thus an increasing sense

of urgency amongst key stakeholders in the industry to ensure that garments/ textile importers and producers in Europe come into compliance with this legislation. There are also trends indicating that European consumers are increasingly demanding that clothes and textiles should not only be produced but also disposed of in a socially and environmentally responsible manner (McKinsey & Co/GFA, 2020).

Criticism has however also been expressed that brands are "not walking the talk" when it comes to circularity. In other words, NGOs, campaign organizations, and critical media coverage has pointed out that the global brands appear to be communicated more about the need for circularity and distinct pilot initiatives on circularity in their value chains (Brydges, 2021). Hence, accusations of "circularity" greenwashing have been widespread concerning brand/retailer communication about their commitment to circularity efforts.

In my view, this raises the question of whether we are indeed seeing a move towards circularity in the global clothing and textile value chains. This must also be seen against existing initiatives and practices for disposing of post-consumption and post-production of textile/garments waste in Europe and South Asia (the geographical region that I am most familiar with). In Europe, mainly charities have been involved in the reuse and resale of clothing/textiles that have been sold to Global North consumers. Increasingly, a number of barriers are instituted in the Global South to importing remaining (excess) clothes from the Global North (Tranberg Hansen and Le Zotte, 2019). In the Global South, there are existing value chains for re-using textile wastes which are turned into new products. Moreover, there are already existing systems for re-using/recycling used clothes (Noman et al., 2013). In fact, local recycling clusters, particularly Panipat in India, are facing increasing challenges as they are not sufficiently upgraded in economic, social, and environmental terms to develop new products that can be re-sold to consumers in the Global South and North (Kapoor and Khare, 2019). Into this pre-existing landscape a range of relatively new companies are seeking to provide new types of technology solutions to recycling thread/clothes and serve as sub-suppliers to the large suppliers in countries in South Asia.

Global brands are latecomers into this pre-existing landscape of reuse, recycling, and resale of textile/clothes waste and relatively little is known about how they (do) not integrate circular economy concerns in their GVCs (Kantt and Pedersen, 2019). In particular, we know little about the different trajectories that different brands and suppliers follow in response to the above-mentioned circular economy imperatives: some being "front-runners" while others apparently do very little or nothing to address circular economy concerns. In addition, we know less about whether circular economy initiatives in this industry/value chain really make a difference in relation to "greening" these value chains or whether this is mainly a form of new "sustainability" rhetoric on the parts of brands and suppliers. Furthermore, we know little about whether there is a dark side to circular economy initiatives in this value chain – for instance, whether post-production waste in countries such as India and Pakistan is being recycled with the help of forced labor or child labor in local production clusters in South Asia.

I think that this calls for more sustained research into whether, and if so why, the European and South Asian garment and textile value chains are (not) being reconfigured in response to circular economy imperatives. Key questions that I would like to see answered include: (a) how do brands and suppliers geographically (re)organize their value chains to dispose of their production and post-consumption textile/apparel waste?; (b) what are the drivers behind/barriers to the engagement of brands and suppliers in circular economy initiatives?; (c) which circular economy rhetorical strategies/discourses are brands and suppliers employing in their value chains?; (d) how do brands and suppliers (not) innovate and organize their circular economy work in their design, marketing, transportation, sourcing, and sustainability activities – both internally within the companies themselves and in their partnerships with other actors?; (e) in turn, how do their circular economy initiatives affect the economic, social, and environmental upgrading/downgrading of suppliers and workers in India and Pakistan?

The theoretical value added of such a research endeavor would be to conceptualize how circular economy drivers, discourses, practices, and impacts are reconfiguring global destruction/recycling networks with particular focus on the European–South Asian apparel/textile industries. If the above questions were investigated empirically, we would also generate new data and insights into these drivers, discourses, practices, and economic/social/environmental up/downgrading impacts of the (postulated) circular economy transition in the European and South Asian garment and textile value chains.

POLICY IMPLICATIONS

How does this book contribute to lessons learned that may inform policymaking and practice in relation to CSR in GVCs?

Implications for Brands and Retailers

First, policymakers and practitioners in this field should not assume that CSR is viewed in a similar way by brands, suppliers, worker representatives, NGOs, and other interested parties throughout the value chain. While this may seem a simple point, it is nevertheless frequently overlooked by many brands, NGOs, and multi-stakeholder initiatives in the Global North. In fact, what is presented as "CSR" is often based on a narrow understanding of the term that is in line with the interests of European and North American brands and retailers. However, such conceptualizations of CSR are not "natural" or "self-evident" in their own right (Riisgaard et al., 2020). They reflect the particular economic interests and imperatives of these brands and retailers that often contradict or are downright out of touch with the interests and every-day realities facing suppliers, workers, NGOs, and trade unions in the Global South. Obviously, the latter stakeholders also have divergent interests and viewpoints. Hence, the implications of value chain actors often having divergent economic interests and visions of CSR may be at least two-fold.

First, unless brands/retailers and multi-stakeholder initiatives in the Global North acknowledge that there may be competing visions of CSR in their value chains, their policies and practices are likely be ineffective. In other words, there may not be any buy-in to their views of CSR, and CSR compliance may become "symbolic" amongst their supplier factories, rather than substantive. A good example of this was displayed in the 2004 documentary, "A Decent Factory," which follows representatives of Nokia, the former world-leading mobile phone brand, as they examine working conditions at a Chinese factory that manufactures products for the company. At one point in the documentary, an auditor employed by Nokia points out to a Chinese manager in the factory that cups for drinking water should not be stored on top of containers of chemicals. The Chinese factory manager agrees and immediately orders his subordinate to remove the chemicals from the toilet area and instead place them in the factory kitchen (Balmes, 2004).

Second, another important implication is that brands/retailers, particularly in their headquarters, need to obtain a better understanding of the socio-cultural and socio-economic contexts where they source their products. Often these brands and retailers have local sourcing offices in production countries that have relatively in-depth understanding of these local production contexts. However, as overall policy- and decision-making typically is dominated by headquarters thousands of miles away, important local perspectives are often not incorporated in "global" CSR policy formulation and subsequent impli- cation. Certainly, there are brands and retailers that have managed to better integrate global and local perspectives on CSR in their work.

However, it still appears as if some corporate and multi-stakeholder initiative policies and programs tend to overlook or simply ignore impor- tant local perspectives on CSR in GVCs. For instance, many brands and multi-stakeholder initiatives are now beginning to adopt policies and goals towards decarbonizing their clothing and textile value chains. They may not place the same emphasis on climate adaptation although this may be a more urgent policy challenge in some local production contexts in the Global South. For instance, flooding may place entire factory areas under water and local neighborhoods inhabited by workers in these neighborhoods may lose their homes overnight. Protecting local factories and workers against this kind of environmental change should – in my view – be at the forefront of the climate change policies and practices of global brands and retailers. Instead, there is a tendency to overlook perspectives and concerns that are critical to local value chain participants.

Another example of how it may be easy to "overlook" important socio-economic and environmental challenges faced by local suppliers and workers relates to the "circular economy" in the clothing and textile industries. Here brands and retailers, often latecomers to debates about circularity, are trying to design and implement circular economy considerations amongst their GVCs. However, little consideration appears to go into mapping existing systems of re-using and recycling clothes in Global South contexts. For instance, in the Pakistani textile city of Faisalabad, Noman et al. (2013) argue that no waste is sent to landfill. Cotton is sold to brick-kilns for use as alternative fuel, iron is sold in local junk markets from where it finds its way to recycling industries, and paper waste is recycled for producing new paper products. Iron and plastic drums are returned to chemical industries for refilling, and cutting rags are used for items such as ropes and underlay. It is also sometimes shredded and employed as fillings in pillows and mattresses. This improves waste management, lowers costs, and minimizes the need for the use of virgin materials. In such examples, it seems ironic that brands and retailers based in the Global North are trying to enhance circularity in their value chains, without being aware of or first properly mapping existing "recycling value chains" in the Global South. Hence, better context and cultural awareness is something that can still be considerably strengthened amongst staff and reflected in the policies and practices of many retailers, brands, and multi-stakeholder initiatives, even if some of these actors are already paying attention to these issues.

Implications for Suppliers

In this book, I have also highlighted the importance of considering supplier perspectives on CSR in GVCs. However, perhaps part of the solutions that suppliers face in relation to CSR in GVCs lie outside the traditional realm of "CSR." Clearly, there is scope for suppliers to enhance their agency in GVCs with the purpose of getting "a better deal" from their participation in these chains. While the cooperative paradigm to CSR in global chains (a buyer-driven model) has long emphasized the importance of trust and long-term trading relations amongst buyers and suppliers, suppliers can also think more strategically about which brands/retailers they work with. Brands and retailers are obviously not the same in their sourcing and CSR policies and practices. Some brands/retailers are much more supportive and committed to their suppliers. In addition, suppliers have the option of not taking orders or collaborating with buyers that are not willing to support their growth and development in the long term. In addition, suppliers can more actively make sure that they only accept orders, which enable them to both earn money and abide by general CSR requirements related to payment of minimum wages, limits to overtime, occupational health and safety, and so on. In other words, suppliers can pro-actively ensure that they do not contribute towards a race-to-the-bottom in their industry.

In a longer-term perspective, it also makes sense for suppliers to try to move up the value chain, moving from manufacturing to establishing their own brands and sell their products, not only domestically but also in international markets. In this way, they will likely be able to increase their profit margins and significantly reduce their dependence on brands and retailers in Europe and North America. Many suppliers in the Global South are already actively avoiding becoming overly dependent on selling their products to buyers in Europe and North America, instead selling these products to growing middle classes in their own countries, or through regional value chains, to other "producer-turned-consumption" countries where local, national, and regional markets for textile, clothing, and other products have been on the rise in recent years (Horner and Nadvi, 2018). At least in theory, they could also attempt to be more pro-active in selling the recycling know-how that these cluster-based suppliers appear to be in possession of.

In the past, the GVC literature emphasized that global brands and retailers would actively support product and process upgrading amongst their suppliers, but that they would also actively prevent suppliers from encroaching on some of their core competences in the areas of marketing and branding (Schmitz, 2006). However, examples from other industries, for instance the global windpower industry, have proved the companies based in the Global South (or East) can move up their value chain and create their own brands, achieving significant market share and influence outside their home countries. In the windpower industry, this applies to companies such as Suzlon (an Indian company) and Goldwind (a Chinese company) that have managed to achieve significant market shares in the global on-shore market for windpower.

Implications for Workers, Labor Unions, and Governments in the Global South

The final value chain actor that I have considered in this book is workers. Here I remain less optimistic for the prospects for CSR becoming a means for enhancing worker organizing and influence in GVCs. The literature on labor agency in GVCs has demonstrated that workers may often gain temporary gains from linking up with labor rights advocates in the Global North. However, given the dynamic nature of GVCs, temporary gains for workers obtained through campaigns, linking up with NGOs or critical press in the Global North are likely to be quickly undermined. Moreover, workers, whether organized through trade unions or unorganized, are unlikely to improve their conditions in GVCs in the long term by forging linkages with CSR-sensitive brands.

In order to fundamentally improve workers' conditions in GVCs, what Oka et al. (2020a) describe as advocacy is required. They mainly refer to global brands trying to influence government rules, regulations, and their implementation in producer countries in the Global South. This type of advocacy is also taken up by international organizations, governments, and NGOs, but perhaps not with the level of success that these actors hope for. At least, many governments in the Global South appear to believe that their economies' continued competitiveness is related to maintaining low wages and suppressing workers' rights.

Thus, the basic challenge remains to commit governments in the Global South that they should actively support the rights of workers to organize, join trade unions, and engage in collective bargaining. Here it will be important to demonstrate the "business case" for social upgrading in local export industries. In other words, that social upgrading may go ahead with achieving greater international competitiveness. In short, it pays off for governments to support the development of an educated workforce, encouraging their freedom of association and right to collective bargaining with the aim of being able to move out of lower value-added industries into more value-added, technology-intensive industries that require a higher level of worker awareness, negotiation abilities, and skills. This will in turn enable producer countries in their industrialization processes, diversify their economies, and become less vulnerable from their participation in GVCs. Hence, I conclude this book by stating that "CSR is not enough" – the way to enhance social and environmental upgrading in GVCs must be seen in the light of local industrialization policies, state commitments to educational achievements, willingness to enforce labor and environmental legislation as an integral part of economic upgrading, and raise overall income levels of citizens in the Global South.

References

Alexander, R. (2016). *Sustainability in global production networks: rethinking buyer-driven governance*, doctoral thesis, Faculty of Humanities, School of Environment, Education, and Development, University of Manchester, Manchester.

Alford, M., Barrientos, S., & Visser, M. (2017). Multi-scalar labor agency in global production networks: contestation and crisis in the South African fruit sector. *Development and Change*, 48(4): 721–745.

Altenburg, T., & Meyer-Stamer, J. (1999). How to promote clusters: policy experiences from Latin America. *World Development*, 27(9): 1693–1713.

Amaeshi, K., & Idemudia, U. (2015). Africapitalism: a management idea for business in Africa? *Africa Journal of Management*, 1(2): 210–223.

Amengual, M., Distelhorst, G., & Tobin, D. (2020). Global purchasing as labor regulation: the Missing Middle. *ILR Review*, 73(4): 817–840.

Anguelov, N. (2015). *The Dirty Side of the Garments Industry – Fast Fashion and Its Negative Impacts on Environment and Society*. London: CRC Press/Taylor & Francis Group.

Anner, M. (2012). Corporate social responsibility and freedom of association rights: the precarious quest for legitimacy and control in global supply chains. *Politics & Society*, 40(4): 609–644.

Anner, M. (2020). Abandoned? The impact of Covid-19 on workers and businesses at the bottom of global garment supply chains. Report. Center for Global Workers' Rights, Pennsylvania State University, April.

Anner, M., Bair, J., & Blasi, J. (2013). Towards joint liability in global supply chains: addressing the root causes of labor violations in international subcontracting networks. *Comparative Labor Law and Policy Journal*, 35(1): 1–43.

Appelbaum, R. (2008). Giant transnational contractors in East Asia: emergent trends in global supply chains. *Competition and Change*, 12(1): 69–87.

Asif, M., Jajja, M.S.S., & Searcy, C. (2019). Social compliance standards: re-evaluating the buyer and supplier perspectives. *Journal of Cleaner Production*, 227: 457–471.

Axfoundation (2020). Axfoundation mobilizes companies to support migrant workers through digital training on COVID-19. Accessed at: https://www.axfoundation.se/en/news/digital-training-covid-19, 9 September 2020.

Azmeh, S., & Nadvi, K. (2014). Asian firms and the restructuring of global value chains. *International Business Review*, 23(4): 708–717.

Bae, J., Lund-Thomsen, P., & Lindgreen, A. (2020). Global value chains and supplier perceptions of corporate social responsibility: a case study of garment manufacturers in Myanmar. *Global Networks*, In Press.

Bair, J., & Palpacuer, F. (2015). CSR beyond the corporation: contested governance in global value chains. *Global Networks*, 15(1): S1–S19.

Bair, J., & Werner, M. (2011). Commodity chains and the uneven geographies of global capitalism: a disarticulations perspective. *Environment and Planning A*, 43(5): 988–997.

Bair, J., Berndt, C., Boeckler, M., & Werner, M. (2013). Dis/articulating producers, markets, and regions: new directions in critical studies of commodity chains. *Environment and Planning A*, 45(11): 2544–2552.

Balmes, T. (2004). *A Decent Factory*. Accessed at: https://thomasbalmes.com/a-decent -factory/, 24 May 2021.

Bansal, P., & Song, H.C. (2017). Similar but not the same: differentiating corporate sustainability from corporate social responsibility. *Academy of Management Journals*, 11(1): 105–149.

Barrientos, S. (2019a). Gender dynamics in global value chains. Chapter 20, in Ponte, S., Gereffi, G., & Raj-Reichert, G. (eds.), *Handbook on Global Value Chains*. Cheltenham, UK and Northampton, MA, USA: Edward Elgar Publishing, pp. 324–338.

Barrientos, S. (2019b). *Changing Gender Patterns of Work in Global Value Chains: Capturing the Gains*. Cambridge: Cambridge University Press.

Barrientos, S., & Smith, S. (2007). Do workers benefit from ethical trade? Assessing codes of labor practice in global production systems. *Third World Quarterly*, 28(4): 713–729.

Barrientos, S., Dolan, C., & Tallontire, A. (2003). A gendered value chain approach to codes of conduct in African horticulture. *World Development*, 31(9): 1511–1526.

Barrientos, S., Gereffi, G., & Rossi, A. (2011). Economic and social upgrading in global production networks: a new paradigm for a changing world. *International Labour Review*, 150(3–4): 319–340.

Barrientos, S., Knorringa, P., Evers, B., Visser, M., & Opondo, M. (2016). Shifting regional dynamics of global value chains: implications for economic and social upgrading in African agriculture. *Environment and Planning A*, 48(7): 1266–1283.

Bartley, T. (2018). *Rules Without Rights: Land, Labor and Private Authority Within the Global Economy*. Oxford: Oxford University Press.

Bartley, T., & Egels-Zandén, N. (2015). Responsibility and neglect in global production networks: the uneven significance of codes of conduct in Indonesian factories. *Global Networks*, 15(S1): S21–S44.

Baur, D., & Schmitz, H.P. (2012). Corporations and NGOs: when accountability leads to co-optation. *Journal of Business Ethics*, 106: 9–21.

BBC News (2020). Coronavirus India: death and despair as migrant workers flee cities. Accessed at: https://www.bbc.com/news/av/world-asia-52776442, 8 September 2020.

Becattini, G. (1990). The Marshallian industrial district as a socio-economic notion, in Pyke, F., Becattini, G., & Sengenberger, W. (eds.), *Industrial Districts and Interfirm Co-operation in Italy*. Geneva: International Institute for Labour Studies, pp. 37–51.

Better Buying (2020). What we do. Accessed at: https://betterbuying.org/what-we-do/ , 12 October 2020.

Blowfield, M.E., & Frynas, J.G. (2005). Editorial setting new agendas: critical perspectives on corporate social responsibility in the developing world. *International Affairs*, 81(3): 499–513.

Böhm, S., Brei, V., & Dabhi, S. (2015). EDF Energy's green CSR claims examined: the follies of global carbon commodity chains. *Global Networks*, 15(1): 87–107.

Bolwig, S., Ponte, S., Du Toit, A., Riisgaard, L., & Halberg, N. (2010). Integrating poverty and environmental concerns into global value chain analysis. *Development Policy Review*, 28(2): 173–194.

Brammer, S., Jackson, G., & Matten, D. (2012). Corporate social responsibility and institutional theory: new perspectives on private governance. *Socio-Economic Review*, 10: 3–28.

Brydges, T. (2021). Closing the loop on take, make, waste: investigating circular economy practices in Swedish fashion industry. *Journal of Cleaner Production*, 293: 126245.

Buhman, K., Taylor, M., & Giuliani, E. (2019). Editorial – business and human rights in global value chains. *Competition and Change*, 23(4): 337–345.

Butler, J. (2006). Performative acts and gender constitution: an essay in phenomenology and feminist theory, in Arnot, M., & Mac An Haill, M. (eds.), *The RoutledgeFalmer Reader in Gender and Education*. Abingdon: Routledge, pp. 61–71.

Butollo, F. (2020). Digitalization and the geographies of production: towards reshoring or global fragmentation. *Competition and Change*, In Press.

Campling, L., & Havice, E. (2019). Bringing the environment into GVC analysis: antecedents and advances. Chapter 12, in Ponte, S., Gereffi, G., & Raj-Reichert, G. (eds.), *Handbook on Global Value Chains*. Cheltenham, UK and Northampton, MA, USA: Edward Elgar Publishing, pp. 214–227.

Candland, C. (2001). The costs of incorporation: labor institutions, industrial restructuring, and new trade union strategies in India and Pakistan, in Candland, C., & Sil, R. (eds.), *The Politics of Labor in a Global Age: Continuity and Change in Late-Industrializing and Post-Soviet Economies*. Oxford: Oxford University Press, pp. 69–94.

Candland, C. (2007). Workers' organizations in Pakistan: why no role in formal conflicts? *Critical Asian Studies*, 39: 35–57.

Carmody, P. (2020). Meta-trends in global value chains and development: interacting impacts with COVID-19 in Africa. *Transnational Corporations Journal*, 27(2): 143–155.

Carswell, G., & De Neve, G. (2013). Labouring for global markets: conceptualising labour agency in Global Production Networks. *Geoforum*, 44: 62–70.

Casaola, T. (2020). Empresas niegan empleo por tener diabetes, hipertensión y obesidad. Animal Político. Accessed at: https://www.animalpolitico.com/ 2020/09/covid-niegan-empleo-enfermos-diabetes-hipertension-obesidad -discriminacion/?s=09&fbclid=IwAR2gA3I7BWaQX67FG-vIzoDENmUZ7r8Xr2 -k2P1sWTwqui5mFQWqpMoMtN4, 24 September 2020.

Cashore, B., Knudsen, J.S., Moon, J., & Van der Ven, H. (2021). Private authority and public interactions in global context: governance spheres for problem-solving. *Regulation and Governance*, 15(4): 1166–1182.

Chan, C.K. (2014). Constrained labour agency and the changing regulatory regime in China. *Development and Change*, 45(4): 685–709.

Channel 4 (2020). Revealed: shocking conditions in PPE supplying factories in the UK. Accessed at: https://www.channel4.com/news/revealed-shocking-conditions-in-ppe -factories-supplying-uk, 9 September 2020.

Cheyns, E. (2014). Making minority voices heard in transnational roundtables: the role of local NGOs in reintroducing justice and attachments. *Agriculture and Human Values*, 31(3): 439–451.

Cline, E.L. (2020). Bangladesh threatens to ban these UK brands, escalating battle to get factories paid. Accessed at: https://www.forbes.com/sites/elizabethlcline/ 2020/05/27/bangladesh-threatens-to-ban-these-uk-brands-escalating-battle-to-get -factories-paid/#2012a8fa15c4, 9 September 2020.

Coalition (2020). Coalition to end forced labor in the Uyghur region, about our coalition. Accessed at: https://enduyghurforcedlabour.org/about/, 7 September 2020.

Coe, N.M. (2021). *Advanced Introduction to Global Production Networks*. Cheltenham, UK and Northampton, MA, USA: Edward Elgar Publishing.

Coe, N., & Hess, M. (2013). Global production networks, labour, and development. *Geoforum*, 44(1): 4–9.

Coe, N.M., & Jordhus-Lier, D.C. (2011). Constrained agency – re-evaluating the geographies of labor. *Progress in Human Geography*, 35(2): 211–233.

Coe, N.M., & Yeung, H. (2015a). Toward a dynamic theory of global production networks. *Economic Geography*, 91(1): 29–58.

Coe, N., & Yeung, H. (2015b). *Global Production Networks: Theorizing Economic Development in an Interconnected World*. Oxford: Oxford University Press.

Coe, N.M., & Yeung, H. (2019). Global production networks: mapping recent conceptual developments. *Journal of Economic Geography*, 19(4): 775–801.

Coe, N., Dicken, P., & Hess, M. (2008). Global production networks: debates and challenges. *Journal of Economic Geography*, 8(3): 271–295.

Corpwatch (2020). Greenwash fact sheet. Accessed at: https://corpwatch.org/article/greenwash-fact-sheet, 6 February 2020.

Coslovsky, S.V. (2014). Flying under the radar? The state and the enforcement of labour laws in Brazil. *Oxford Development Studies*, 42(2): 190–216.

Cumbers, A., Nativel, C., & Routledge, P. (2008). Labour agency and union positionalities in global production networks. *Journal of Economic Geography*, 8(3): 369–387.

Dallas, M.P., Ponte, S., & Sturgeon, T.J. (2019). Power in global value chains. *Review of International Political Economy*, 26(4): 666–694.

Danish Ethical Trading Initiative (2020). The state of ethical trade in Denmark: 2020 (Etisk Handel 2020). Danish Ethical Trading Initiative, Copenhagen.

Danish, M., & Khattak, A. (2020). Economic and social upgrading of firms in football global value chains. *Journal of Distribution Science*, 18(4): 97–106.

Danwatch (2020). Child labour found in Fairtrade cocoa plantations. Accessed at: https://danwatch.dk/en/undersoegelse/child-labour-found-in-fairtrade-cocoa-plantations/, 9 September 2020.

D'Cruz, P., Delannon, N., McCarthy, L., Kourula, A., Moon, J., & Spence, L.J. (2021). Contesting social responsibilities of business: experiences in context. *Human Relations Special Issue* Call for Papers. Accessed at: https://journals.sagepub.com/pb-assets/cmscontent/HUM/HR%20SI%20ContestingSocialResponsibilities%20CFP%20Final-1608661708207.pdf, 15 December 2021.

De Bakker, F., Rasche, A., & Ponte, S. (2019). Multi-stakeholder initiatives on sustainability: a cross-disciplinary review and research agenda for business ethics. *Business Ethics Quarterly*, 29(3): 343–383.

De Neve, G. (2014). Fordism, flexible specialization, and CSR: how Indian garment workers critique neoliberal labour regimes. *Ethnography*, 15(2): 184–207.

Distelhorst, G., Hainmuller, J., & Locke, R.M. (2016). Does lean improve labor standards? Capability building and social performance in the Nike supply chain. *Management Science*, 63(3): 707–728.

Distelhorst, G., Locke, R., Pal, T., & Samel, H. (2015). Production goes global, compliance stays local – private regulation in the global electronics industry. *Regulation and Governance*, 9(3): 224–242.

EEA (2019). *Textiles In Europe's Circular Economy*, Briefing no. 10/2019, European Environment Agency, Copenhagen.

Egels-Zandén, N. (2007). Suppliers' compliance with MNCs' codes of conduct: behind the scenes at Chinese toy suppliers. *Journal of Business Ethics*, 75(1): 45–62.

Elson, D., & Pearson, D. (1981). 'Nimble fingers make cheap workers': an analysis of women's employment in Third World manufacturing. *Feminist Review*, 7(1): 87–107.

Ethical Trading Initiative (ETI) (2020). *COVID-19 Briefing Note: Migrant Workers*. London: ETI.

European Coalition for Corporate Justice (2020). Commissioner Reynders announces EU corporate due diligence legislation, Brussels: ECCJ. Accessed at: https:// corporatejustice.org/news/16806-commissioner-reynders-announces-eu-corporate -due-diligence-legislation, 9 September 2020.

European Commission (EC) (2011). *A Renewed EU Strategy 2011–2014 for Corporate Social Responsibility*. Brussels: European Commission.

European Communities (EC) (2001). *Promoting a European Framework for Corporate Social Responsibility*. Brussels: European Communities.

European Parliament (2021). European Parliament resolution of 10 March 2021 with recommendations to the Commission on corporate due diligence and corporate accountability, Brussels: European Parliament. Accessed at: https://www.europarl .europa.eu/doceo/document/TA-9-2021-0073_EN.html, 21 May 2021.

Fichter, M., & McCallum, J.K. (2015). Implementing global framework agreements: the limits of social partnership. *Global Networks*, 15(1): 65–85.

FMC (2006). *Working Together Works – Cluster Case Studies*. New Delhi: FMC.

Gansemans, A., & D'Haese, M. (2019). Staying under the radar: constraints on labour agency of pineapple plantation workers in Costa Rica. *Agriculture and Human Values*, 37(2): 397–414.

Gereffi, G. (2019). Economic upgrading in global value chains. Chapter 14, in Ponte, S., Gereffi, G., & Raj-Reichert, G. (eds.), *Handbook on Global Value Chains*. Cheltenham, UK and Northampton, MA, USA: Edward Elgar Publishing, pp. 240–254.

Gereffi. G. (2020). What does the COVID-19 pandemic teach us about global value chains? The case of medical supplies. *Journal of International Business Policy*, 3(3): 287–301.

Gereffi, G., & Lee, J. (2016). Economic and social upgrading in global value chains and industrial clusters: why governance matters? *Journal of Business Ethics*, 133(1): 25–38.

Gereffi, G., Humphrey, J., & Sturgeon, T. (2005). The governance of global value chains. *Review of International Political Economy*, 12(1): 78–104.

Giuliani, E. (2016). Human rights and corporate social responsibility in developing countries' industrial clusters. *Journal of Business Ethics*, 133(1): 39–54.

Goger, A. (2013). The making of a 'business case' for environmental upgrading: Sri Lanka's eco-factories. *Geoforum*, 47: 73–83.

Gold, S., Trautims, A., & Trodd, Z. (2015). Modern slavery challenges to supply chain management. *Supply Chain Management: An International Journal*, 20(5): 485–494.

Gond, J.P., Kang, N., & Moon, J. (2011). The government of self-regulation: on the comparative dynamics of corporate social responsibility. *Economy and Society*, 40: 640–671.

Graz, J.C., Helmerich, N., & Prébandier, C. (2020). Hybrid production regimes and labor agency in transnational private governance. *Journal of Business Ethics*, 162(2): 307–362.

Grosser, K. (2016). Corporate social responsibility and multi-stakeholder governance: pluralism, feminist perspectives and women's NGOs. *Journal of Business Ethics*, 137(1): 65–81.

Grosser, K., & McCarthy, L. (2018). Imagining new feminist futures: how feminist social movements contest the neoliberalization of feminism in an increasingly corporate-dominated world. *Gender, Work & Organization*. Epub ahead of print 8 June 2018. DOI: https://doi.org/10.1111/gwao.12267.

Guarin, A., & Knorringa, P. (2014). New middle-class consumers in rising powers: responsible consumption and private standards. *Oxford Development Studies*, 42(2): 151–171.

Gulati, M., Lund-Thomsen, P., & Suresh, S. (2018). Cluster matters: corporate social responsibility and micro, small and medium-sized enterprise clusters in India, in Spence, L., Frynas, J.G., Muthuri, J.N., & Navare, J. (eds.), *Research Handbook on Small Business Social Responsibility*. Cheltenham, UK and Northampton, MA, USA: Edward Elgar Publishing, pp. 77–100.

Gunawardana, S., & Biyanwila, J. (2008). Trade unions in Sri Lanka – beyond party politics, in Benson, J., & Zhu, Y. (eds.), *Trade Unions in Asia: An Economic and Sociological Analysis*. London: Routledge, pp. 177–198.

Gutelius, B. (2015). Disarticulating distribution: labor segmentation and subcontracting in global logistics. *Geoforum*, 60: 53–61.

Henderson, J., Dicken, P., Hess, M., Coe, N.M., & Yeung, H.W-C. (2002). Global production networks and the analysis of economic development. *Review of International Political Economy*, 9: 436–464.

Hobbes, M. (2015). Myth of the ethical shopper. *The Huffington Post*, July. Accessed at: http://highline.huffingtonpost.com/articles/en/the-myth-of-the-ethical-shopper/, 13 October 2015.

Hoffman, P.S., Wu, B., & Liu, K. (2014). Collaborative socially responsible practices for improving the position of Chinese workers in global supply chains. *Journal of Current Chinese Affairs*, 43(3): 111–143.

Horner, R. (2016). A new economic geography of trade and development? Governing south–south trade, value chains, and production networks. *Territory, Politics, and Governance*, 4(4): 400–420.

Horner, R. (2017). Beyond facilitator? State roles in global value chains and global production networks. *Geography Compass*, 11(2): e12307.

Horner, R., & Nadvi, K. (2018). Global production and the rise of the Global South: unpacking 21st century polycentric trade. *Global Networks*, 18(2): 207–237.

Hughes, A. (2001). Multi-stakeholder approaches to ethical trade: towards a reorganisation of UK retailers' global supply chains? *Journal of Economic Geography*, 1(4): 421–437.

Humphrey, J., & Schmitz, H. (2002). How does insertion in global value chains affect industrial clusters? *Regional Studies*, 36(9): 1017–1027.

Huq, R. (2021). How can we ensure that responsible business conduct legislation levels the playing field in practice? Voices from the Forum, OECD Forum on Due Diligence in the Garment and Footwear Sector, Online Conference. Accessed at: http://mneguidelines.oecd.org/forum-on-due-diligence-in-the-garment-and-footwear-sector.htm, 28 April 2021.

Hussein-Khaliq, S. (2004). Eliminating child labour from the Sialkot soccer ball industry – two industry led approaches. *Journal of Corporate Citizenship*, 13: 101–107.

Husselbee, D. (2000). NGOs as development partners to the corporates: child football stitchers in Pakistan. *Development in Practice*, 10(3–4): 377–389.

IDH (2009). *Beyond Auditing: Tapping the Full Potential of Labor Standards Promotion*. Amsterdam: DIEH.

Impactt (2011). *Finding the Sweet Spot: Smarter Ethical Trade that Delivers More for All*. London: Impactt.

International Labor Rights Forum (ILRF) (2010). *Missed the Goal for Workers: The Reality of Football Stitchers in India, Pakistan, China, and Thailand*. Washington, DC: ILRF.

International Labour Organization (ILO) (2021). Sustaining peace through decent work: the role of social partners and social dialogue. Accessed at: https://www .ilo.org/global/topics/employment-promotion/recovery-and-reconstruction/WCMS _824971/lang--en/index.htm, 17 December 2021.

Jalali, R. (2008). International funding of NGOs in India. *Voluntas*, 19(2): 161–188.

Jamali, D. (2010). The CSR of MNC subsidiaries in developing countries: global, local, substantive or diluted? *Journal of Business Ethics*, 93(2): 181–200.

Jamali, D., Lund-Thomsen, P., & Jeppesen, S. (2017). SMEs and CSR in developing countries. *Business and Society*, 56(1): 11–22.

Jammulamadaka, N. (2015). Responsibility for the third world factory: limits of Eurocentric CSR and making room for the state. *Decision*, 42(1): 71–82.

Jenkins, K. (2014). Women, mining and development: an emerging research agenda. *The Extractive Industries and Society*, 1(2): 329–339.

Junaid, M., Malik, R.N., & De-Sheng, P. (2017). Health hazards of child labor in the leather products and surgical instruments manufacturing of Sialkot, Pakistan. *Environmental Pollution*, 226: 198–211.

Kabeer, N. (2000). *Power to Choose: Bangladeshi Women and Labour Market Decisions in London and Dhaka*. London: Verso.

Kantt, K., & Pedersen, E.R. (2019). Toward a circular economy of fashion: experiences from a brand's product take-back initiative. *Journal of Fashion and Marketing*, 23(3): 345–365.

Kaplinsky, R. (2005). *Globalization, Poverty and Inequality*. Cambridge: Polity Press.

Kapoor, A., & Khare, A.K. (2019). The afterlife of discarded woolens: who is recycling my clothes? *International Journal of Management*, 10(5): 84–98.

Khalid, M.K., Agha, M.H., Shah, S.T.H., & Akhtar, M.N. (2020). Conceptualizing audit fatigue in the context of sustainable supply chains. *Sustainability*, 12(21): 9135.

Khan, A. (2007). *Representing Children – Power, Policy and the Discourse on Child Labour in the Football Manufacturing Industry of Sialkot*. Karachi, Pakistan: Oxford University Press.

Khan, F.R. (2007). Representational approaches matter. *Journal of Business Ethics*, 73: 77–89.

Khan, F.R., & Lund-Thomsen, P. (2011). CSR as imperialism: towards a phenomeno-logical approach to CSR in the developing world. *Journal of Change Management*, 11(1): 73–90.

Khan, M., Ponte, S., & Lund-Thomsen, P. (2020). 'The factory manager dilemma': purchasing practices and environmental upgrading in apparel global value chains. *Environment and Planning A: Economy and Space*, 52(4): 766–789.

Khara, N., & Lund-Thomsen, P. (2012). Value chain restructuring, work organization, and labor outcomes in football manufacturing in India. *Competition and Change*, 16(4): 261–280.

Knight, G., & Greenberg, J. (2002). Promotionalism and subpolitics: Nike and its labor critics. *Management Communication Quarterly*, 15(4): 541–570.

Knorringa, P. (1999). Agra: an old cluster facing the new competition. *World Development*, 27(9): 1587–1604.

Knorringa, P., & Nadvi, K. (2016). Rising power clusters and the challenges of local and global standards. *Journal of Business Ethics*, 133(1): 55–72.

Krauss, J., & Krishnan, A. (2016). *Global decisions and local realities: priorities and producers' upgrading opportunities in agricultural global production networks*, UNFSS Working Paper no. 7, Geneva: United Nations Forum for Sustainability Standards.

Krishnan, A. (2018). *Rethinking the environmental dimensions of upgrading and embeddedness in production networks: the case of Kenyan horticulture farmers*, PhD thesis, Global Development Institute, School of Environment, Education, and Development, University of Manchester.

Krueger, P., Sautner, Z., & Starks, L. (2020). The importance of climate risks for investors. *The Review of Financial Studies*, 33(3): 1087–1111.

Kumar, A. (2019). A race to the bottom – lessons from a workers' struggle at a Bangalore warehouse. *Competition and Change*, 23(4): 346–377.

Lebaron, G., & Lister, J. (2015). Benchmarking global supply chains: the power of the 'ethical audit' regime. *Review of International Studies*, 41(5): 905–924.

Leitheiser, E., Hossain, S.N., Sen, S.N., Tasnim, G., Moon, J., Knudsen, J.S., & Rahman, S. (2020). *Early impacts of Coronavirus on Bangladesh apparel supply chains*, RISC Report, Copenhagen Business School, April.

Levy, D. (2008). Political contestation in global production networks. *Academy of Management Review*, 33(4): 943–963.

Locke, R. (2013). *The Promise and Limits of Private Power – Promoting Labor Standards in a Global Economy*. Cambridge: Cambridge University Press.

Locke, R., & Romis, M. (2010). The promise and perils of private voluntary regulation – labor standards and work organization in two Mexican factories. *Review of International Political Economy*, 17(1): 45–74.

Locke, R.M., Amengual, M., & Mangla, A. (2009). Virtue out of necessity: compliance, commitment, and the improvement of labor standards. *Politics & Society*, 37(3): 319–351.

Lund-Thomsen, P. (2008). The global sourcing and codes of conduct debate: five myths and five recommendations. *Development and Change*, 39(6): 1005–1018.

Lund-Thomsen, P. (2013). Labor agency in the football manufacturing industry of Sialkot, Pakistan. *Geoforum*, 44(1): 71–81.

Lund-Thomsen, P. (2020). Corporate social responsibility: a supplier-centered perspective. *Environment and Planning A*, 52(8): 1700–1709.

Lund-Thomsen, P., & Coe, N. (2015). Corporate social responsibility and labor agency: the case of Nike in Pakistan. *Journal of Economic Geography*, 15(2): 275–296.

Lund-Thomsen, P., & Lindgreen, A. (2014). CSR in global value chains. Where are we now? Where are we going? *Journal of Business Ethics*, 123(1): 11–22.

Lund-Thomsen, P., & Lindgreen, A. (2018). Is there a sweet spot in ethical trade? A critical appraisal of the potential for aligning buyer, supplier and worker interests in global production networks. *Geoforum*, 90: 84–90.

Lund-Thomsen, P., & Lindgreen, A. (2020). Corporate social responsibility in global value chains: where are we now? Where are we going?, in Lund-Thomsen, P., Hansen, M.W., & Ponte, S. (eds.), *Business and Development Studies: Issues and Perspectives*. Abingdon: Routledge, pp. 159–179.

Lund-Thomsen, P., & Nadvi, K. (2010a). Global value chains, local collective action and corporate social responsibility: a review of empirical evidence. *Business Strategy and the Environment*, 19(1): 1–13.

Lund-Thomsen, P., & Nadvi, K. (2010b). Clusters, chains, and compliance: corporate social responsibility and governance in football manufacturing in South Asia. *Journal of Business Ethics*, 93(Suppl. 2): 201–222.

Lund-Thomsen, P., & Nadvi, K. (2012). Applying the Atlanta Agreement, in Utting, P., Reed, D., & Mukherjee Reed, A. (eds.), *Business Regulation and Non-state Actors: Whose Standards? Whose Development?* London: Routledge/UNRISD, pp. 189–200.

Lund-Thomsen, P., & Ramirez, J. (2020). *Beyond compliance and cooperation? Rethinking corporate social responsibility in global value chains in the age of COVID-19*, CBDS Working Paper no. 2020/4, Center for Business and Development Studies, Copenhagen Business School.

Lund-Thomsen, P., Lindgreen, A., & Vanhamme, J. (2016). Industrial clusters and corporate social responsibility in developing countries. What we know, what we don't, and what we need to know. *Journal of Business Ethics*, 133(1): 9–24.

Lund-Thomsen, P., Nadvi, K., Chan, A., Khara, N., & Xue, H. (2012). Labor in global value chains: work conditions in football manufacturing in China, India, and Pakistan. *Development and Change*, 43(6): 1211–1237.

Lund-Thomsen, P., Riisgaard, L., Coe, N.M., Singh, S., & Ghori, S. (2018). *Bridging global standard requirements and local farmer needs: implementing partners of the Better Cotton Initiative in Pakistan and India*, CBDS Working Paper Series, No. 1, Center for Business and Development Studies, Copenhagen Business School.

Lund-Thomsen, P., Riisgaard, L., Ghori, S., Singh, S., & Coe, N.M. (2021). Global value chains and intermediaries in multi-stakeholder initiatives in Pakistan and India. *Development and Change*, In Press.

Marslev, K. (2020). *The political economy of social upgrading – a class relational analysis of social and economic trajectories of the garments industries of Cambodia and Vietnam*, PhD thesis, Department of Social Sciences and Business, Roskilde University/Danish Institute of Human Rights, Copenhagen.

Matten, D., & Moon, J. (2008). 'Implicit' and 'explicit' CSR: a conceptual framework for a comparative understanding of corporate social responsibility. *Academy of Management Review*, 33(2): 404–424.

Mayes, R. (2015). A social license to operate: corporate social responsibility, local communities and the constitution of global production networks. *Global Networks*, 15(1): 109–128.

McCarthy, L. (2017). Empowering women through corporate social responsibility: a feminist Foucauldian perspective. *Business Ethics Quarterly*, 27(4): 603–631.

McCarthy, L., & Moon, J. (2018). Disrupting the gender institution: conscious-raising in the cocoa value chain. *Organization Studies*, 39(9): 1153–1177.

McCarthy, L., Soundararajan, V., & Taylor, S. (2020). The hegemony of men in global value chains: why it matters for labour governance. *Human Relations*, 74(12): 2051–2074.

McKinsey & Co/GFA (2020). *Fashion on Climate – How the Fashion Industry Can Urgently Act to Reduce Its Greenhouse Gas Emissions*. Copenhagen: Global Fashion Agenda.

Merk, J. (2014). The rise of tier 1 firms in the global garment industry: challenges for labor rights advocates. *Oxford Development Studies*, 42(2): 259–277.

Mezzadri, A. (2014a). Backshoring, local sweatshop regimes and CSR in India. *Competition & Change*, 18(4): 327–344.

Mezzadri, A. (2014b). Indian garment clusters and CSR norms: incompatible agendas at the bottom of the garment commodity chain. *Oxford Development Studies*, 42(2): 238–258.

Mezzadri, A. (2016). Class, gender and the sweatshop: on the nexus between labour commodification and exploitation. *Third World Quarterly*, 37(10): 1877–1900.

Mezzadri, A., & Fan, L. (2018). 'Classes of labour' at the margins of global commodity chains in India and China. *Development and Change*, 49(4): 1034–1063.

Miller, D. (2012). *Last Nightshift in Savar: The Story of the Spectrum Sweater Factory Collapse*. Alnwick: McNidder and Grace.

Mitkidis, K., Perkovic, S., & Mitkidis, P. (2019). Tendencies in contractual governance to promote human and labor rights in transnational supply chains. *Competition and Change*, 23(4): 397–419.

Montiel, I. (2008). Corporate social responsibility and corporate sustainability: separate pasts, common future. *Organization and Environment*, 21(3): 245–269.

Moon, J., & Knudsen, J.S. (2021). Corporate social responsibility and government: the role of discretion for engagement with public policy. *Business Ethics Quarterly*, In Press.

Morton, J. (2020). On the susceptibility and vulnerability of agricultural value chains to COVID-19. *World Development*, 136, In Print.

Motsei, N., & Nkomo, S.M. (2016). Antecedents of bullying in the South African workplace: societal context matters. *Africa Journal of Management*, 2(1): 50–72.

Munir, K., Ayaz, M., Levy, D.L., & Willmott, H. (2018). The role of intermediaries in governance of global production networks: restructuring work relations in Pakistan's apparel industry. *Human Relations*, 71(4): 560–583.

Nadvi, K. (1999). Shifting ties: social networks in the surgical instrument cluster of Sialkot, Pakistan. *Development and Change*, 30(1): 141–175.

Nadvi, K. (2014). Rising powers and labour and environmental standards. *Oxford Development Studies*, 42(2): 137–150.

Nadvi, K. (2016). What role for small enterprises? Industrial clusters, industrial policy and poverty reduction, in Weiss, J., & Tribe, M. (eds.), *Routledge Handbook on Industry and Development*. London: Routledge, pp. 116–134.

Nadvi, K., & Barrientos, S. (2004). *Industrial Clusters and Poverty Reduction and Towards a Methodology for Poverty and Social Impact Assessment of Cluster Development Initiatives*. Vienna: UNIDO.

Naz, F., & Bögenhold, D. (2020). *Unheard Voices: Women, Work, and the Political Economy of Global Production*. London: Palgrave Macmillan.

Neilson, J., & Pritchard, B. (2009). *Value Chain Struggles: Institutions and Governance in the Plantations of South India*. Gloucester: Wiley-Blackwell.

Neilson, J., & Pritchard, B. (2010). Fairness and ethicality in their place: the regional dynamics of fair trade and ethical sourcing agendas in the plantation districts of south India. *Environment and Planning A*, 42(8): 1833–1851.

Nickow, A. (2015). Growing in value: NGOs, social movements and the cultivation of developmental value chains in Uttarakhand, India. *Global Networks*, 15(1): 45–64.

Noman, M., Batool, S.A., & Chaudhury, M.N. (2013). Economic and employment potential in textile waste management in Faisalabad. *Waste Management and Research*, 31(5): 485–493.

OECD (2018). *OECD Due Diligence Guidance for Responsible Business Conduct*. Paris: OECD.

Oka, C., Egels-Zandén, N., & Alexander, R. (2020a). Buyer engagement and labor conditions in global supply chains: the Bangladesh Accord and beyond. *Development and Change*, 51(5): 1306–1330.

Oka, C., Egels-Zandén, N., Rahman, S., & Alexander, R. (2020b). *Scale Matters: Scalability of Business Case Sustainability Initiatives in the Garments Industry*. Royal Holloway: University of London.

Oseland, S.E., Haarstad, H., & Floysand, A. (2012). Labor agency and the importance of the national scale: emergent aquaculture unionism in Chile. *Political Geography*, 31: 94–103.

Oxfam (2010). Better jobs in better supply chains, Briefings for Business no. 5. Oxford: Oxfam.

Pasquali, G., Godfrey, S., & Nadvi, K. (2020). Understanding regional value chains through the interaction of public and private governance: insights from Southern Africa's apparel sector. *Journal of International Business Policy*, 4(3): 368–389.

Patil, R.A., Ghiselli, P., & Ramakrishna, S. (2020). Towards sustainable business strategies for a circular economy: environmental, social and governance (ESG) performance and evaluation, in Liu, L., & Ramakrishna, S. (eds.), *Introduction to Circular Economy*. Singapore: Springer, pp. 527–544.

Perry, P., Wood, S., & Fernie, J. (2015). Corporate social responsibility in garment sourcing networks: factory management perspectives on ethical trade in Sri Lanka. *Journal of Business Ethics*, 130(3): 107–136.

Pickles, J., Barrientos, S., & Knorringa, P. (2016). New end markets, supermarket expansion and shifting social standards. *Environment and Planning A*, 48(7): 1284–1301.

Ponte, S. (2019). *Business, Power and Sustainability in a World of Global Value Chains*. London: Zed Books.

Ponte, S. (2020). Green capital accumulation: business and sustainability management in a world of global value chains. *New Political Economy*, 25(1): 72–84.

Ponte, S., Gereffi, G., & Raj-Reichert, G. (2019). *Handbook on Global Value Chains*. Cheltenham, UK and Northampton, MA, USA: Edward Elgar Publishing.

Porter, M.E., & Kramer, M.F. (2011). Creating shared value. *Harvard Business Review*, 89(1–2): 62–77.

Prieto-Carron, M. (2006). Corporate social responsibility in Latin America: Chiquita, women banana workers and structural inequalities. *Journal of Corporate Citizenship*, 21: 85–95.

Prieto-Carron, M. (2008). Women workers, industrialization, global supply chains, and corporate codes of conduct. *Journal of Business Ethics*, 83(1): 5–17.

Puppim de Oliveira, J., & Jabbour, C. (2017). Environmental management, climate change, CSR and governance of clusters of small firms from developing countries – towards an analytical framework. *Business and Society*, 56(1): 130–151.

Pyke, F., & Lund-Thomsen, P. (2016). Social upgrading in developing country industrial clusters: a reflection on the literature. *Competition and Change*, 20(1): 53–68.

Pyke, F., Becattini, G., & Sengenberger, W. (1990). *Industrial Districts and Inter-firm Co-operation in Italy*. Geneva: International Institute for Labour Studies.

Pyle, A. (2020). How to make remote monitoring work, Webinar 30 June, 13.00 British Standard Time. Impactt, London.

Raj-Reichert, G. (2013). Safeguarding labour in distant factories: health and safety governance in an electronics global production network. *Geoforum*, 44: 23–31.

Rankin, R. (2020). Social compliance auditing during and after COVID-19. Accessed at: https://www.just-style.com/comment/social-compliance-auditing-during-and-after-covid-19_id138647.aspx, 9 September 2020.

Rasche, A., Morsing, M., & Moon, J. (2017). *Corporate Social Responsibility: Strategy, Communication, Governance.* Cambridge: Cambridge University Press.

Reed, D., & McMurtry, J.J. (2009). *Co-operatives in a Global Economy: The Challenges of Cooperating Across Borders.* Newcastle upon Tyne: Cambridge Scholars Publishing.

Rein, M., & Stott, L. (2009). Working together – critical perspectives on six cross-sector partnerships in Southern Africa. *Journal of Business Ethics*, 90: 79–89.

Riisgaard, L. (2009). Global value chains, labor organization and private social standards: lessons from East African cut flower industries. *World Development*, 37: 326–340.

Riisgaard, L., & Hammer, N. (2011). Prospects for labour in global value chains: labour standards in the cut flower and banana industries. *British Journal of Industrial Relations*, 49: 168–190.

Riisgaard, L., Bolwig, S., Ponte, S., Du Toit, A., Halberg, N., & Matose, F. (2010). Integrating poverty and environmental concerns into value chain analysis: a strategic framework and a practical guide. *Development Policy Review*, 28(2): 195–216.

Riisgaard, L., Lund-Thomsen, P., & Coe, N.M. (2020). Multistakeholder initiatives in global production networks: naturalizing specific understandings of sustainability through the Better Cotton Initiative. *Global Networks*, 20(2): 211–236.

Rina (2020). Measuring COVID-19 impact through direct worker reporting. Accessed at: https://www.rina.org/en/business/certification/compliance-social-accountability/coronavirus-impact-workers-reporting, 9 September 2020.

Ruwanpura, K. (2012). Ethical codes – reality and rhetoric? A study of Sri Lanka's apparel industry, geography and environment. Hampshire: University of Southampton.

Ruwanpura, K. (2015). Garments without guilt: uneven labor geographies and ethical trading – Sri Lankan perspectives. *Journal of Economic Geography*, 16(2): 423–446.

Ruwanpura, K. (2016). Scripted performances? Local readings of global health and safety standards (the apparel sector in Sri Lanka), in Nathan, D., Tewari, M., & Sarkar, S. (eds.), *Labor in Global Value Chains in Asia.* Cambridge: Cambridge University Press, pp. 265–288.

Ruwanpura, K., & Hughes, A. (2016). Empowered spaces? Management articulations of gendered spaces in apparel factories in Karachi, Pakistan. *Gender, Place and Culture: A Journal of Feminist Geography*, 23(9): 1270–1285.

Ruwanpura, K., & Wrigley, N. (2011). The costs of compliance: views of Sri Lankan apparel manufacturers in times of global economic crisis. *Journal of Economic Geography*, 11(6): 1031–1049.

Sachdeva, A., & Panfil, O. (2008). *CSR perceptions and activities of small and medium enterprises (SMEs) in seven geographical clusters – survey report.* Vienna: United Nations Industrial Development Organization.

Safire, W. (2008). *Safire's Political Dictionary.* Oxford: Oxford University Press.

Said-Allsopp, M., & Tallontire, A. (2015). Pathways to empowerment?: dynamics of women's participation in global value chains. *Journal of Cleaner Production*, 107: 114–121.

Sandee, H. (2002). The impact of the crisis on small-scale enterprises in Java, findings from selected case studies, in van Dijk, M.P., & Sandee, H. (eds.), *Innovation and*

Small Enterprises in the Third World. Cheltenham, UK and Northampton, MA, USA: Edward Elgar Publishing, Chapter 9.

Scherer, A., Palazzo, G., & Matten, D. (2014). The business firm as a political actor: a new theory of the firm for a globalized world. *Business & Society*, 53(2): 143–156.

Schilling-Vacaflor, A. (2021). Putting the French duty of vigilance law in context: towards corporate accountability for human rights violations in the Global South. *Human Rights Review*, 22(1): 109–127.

Schmitz, H. (2006). Learning and earning in global garment and footwear chains. *The European Journal of Development Research*, 18(4): 546–571.

Schmitz, H., & Nadvi, K. (1999). Clustering and industrialization: introduction. *World Development*, 27(9): 1503–1514.

Schouten, G., & Bitzer, V. (2015). The emergence of southern standards in agricultural value chains: a new trend in sustainability governance?, *Ecological Economics*, 120: 175–184.

Selwyn, B. (2008). Bringing social relations back in: (re)conceptualizing the 'Bullwhip Effect' in global commodity chains. *International Journal of Management Concepts and Philosophy*, 3: 156–175.

Selwyn, B. (2009). Labour flexibility in export horticulture: a case study of Northeast Brazilian grape production. *The Journal of Peasant Studies*, 36: 761–782.

Sharma, D., & Kaps, F.D. (2021). Human rights due diligence legislation in Europe: implications for supply chains in India and Pakistan, New York. Accessed at: https://www.dlapiper.com/en/us/insights/ publications/2021/03/human-rights-due-diligenc e-legislation-in-europe/, DLA Piper Publications, 14 May 2021.

Siegmann, K.A. (2008). Soccer ball production for Nike. *Economic and Political Weekly*, 43: 57–64.

Silver, B. (2003). *Forces of Labour: Workers Movements and Globalization Since 1870.* Cambridge: Cambridge University Press.

Sommer, C. (2017). Drivers and constraints for adopting sustainability standards in small and medium-sized enterprises, Discussion Paper, No. 21/2017, Deutsche Institut for Entwicklungspolitik, Bonn.

SOMO (2020). Responsible disengagement in the time of corona, SOMO/ECCHR/PAX Position Paper, European Center for Constitutional and Human Rights, Berlin.

Sportel, T. (2013). Agency within a socially regulated labour market – a study of unorganized agricultural labour in Kerala. *Geoforum*, 47: 42–52.

Sunley, P. (1999). Space for stakeholding? Stakeholder capitalism and economic geography. *Environment and Planning A*, 31: 2189–2205.

Tallontire, A., Dolan, C., Smith, S. et al. (2005). Reaching the marginalised? Gender value chains and ethical trade in African horticulture. *Development in Practice*, 15(3–4): 559–571.

Tendler, J. (2002). Small firms, the informal sector and the devil's deal. *IDS Bulletin*, 33(3): 1–15.

Thrandardottir, E., & Mitra, S.G. (2019). Who does Greenpeace India represent? Placing limits on the power of INGOs? *Global Governance: A Review of Multilateral and International Organizations*, 25(4): 587–619.

Tokatli, N., Wrigley, N., & Kizilgun, O. (2008). Shifting global supply networks and fast fashion: made in Turkey for Marks & Spencer. *Global Networks*, 8(3): 261–280.

Tran, A. (2011). Corporate social responsibility in socialist Vietnam – implementation, challenges, and local solutions, in Chan, A. (ed.), *Labour in Vietnam*. Singapore: Institute of South East Asian Studies, pp. 119–159.

Tran, A., & Jeppesen, S. (2016). SMEs in their own right: the views of managers and workers in Vietnamese textile, garments, and footwear companies. *Journal of Business Ethics*, 137(3): 589–608.

Tranberg Hansen, K., & Le Zotte, J. (2019). Changing secondhand economies. *Business History*, 61(1): 1–16.

UK-ETI (2017). About ETI. Accessed at: http://www.ethicaltrade.org/about-eti, 13 July 2017.

UK-ETI (2021). Ethical trade during COVID-19. Accessed at: https://www.ethicaltrade .org/, 20 January 2021.

UNIDO (2019). Mainstreaming gender in cluster development, United Nations Industrial Development Organization, Vienna.

Van der Ven, H., Sun, X., & Cashore, B. (2021). Sustainable commodity governance and the global south. *Ecological Economics*, 186, In Press.

Van Kalmthout, D.V., Romeo-Stuppy, K., Huber, L., & Van Eichborn, C. (2021). Mandatory environmental and human rights due diligence. *Tobacco Induced Diseases*, 19(19). Accessed at: https://www.ncbi.nlm.nih.gov/pmc/articles/ PMC7983222/, 21 May 2021.

Ward, H. (2003). Legal issues in corporate citizenship – prepared for the Swedish partnership for global responsibility, International Institute for Environment and Development, London.

Werner, M., & Bair, J. (2011). Guest editorial – commodity chains and the uneven geographies of global capitalism: a disarticulations perspective. *Environment and Planning A*, 43(5): 988–997.

Werner, M., & Bair, J. (2019). Global value chains and uneven development: a disarticulations perspective. Chapter 10, in Ponte, S., Gereffi, G., & Raj-Reichert, G. (eds.), *Handbook on Global Value Chains*. Cheltenham, UK and Northampton, MA, USA: Edward Elgar Publishing, pp. 183–198.

Wills, J. (1999). Managing European works councils in British firms. *Human Resource Management Journal*, 9: 19–38.

Wills, J. (2000). Great expectations: three years in the life of a European works council. *European Journal of Industrial Relations*, 6: 86–105.

Wills, J. (2001). Uneven geographies of capital and labour: lessons of European works councils. *Antipode*, 33: 484–509.

Workers' Rights Consortium (2020). COVID-19 tracker: which brands are acting responsibly towards suppliers and workers? Accessed at: https://www.workersrights .org/issues/covid-19/tracker/, 7 September 2020.

Wright, E.O. (2000). Working class power, capitalist-class interests, and class compromise. *American Journal of Sociology*, 105: 957–1002.

WTO (2021). Trade and labour standards. World Trade Organization, Geneva. Accessed at: https://www.wto.org/english/thewto_e/minist_e/min99_e/english/ about_e/18lab_e.htm, 14 March 2021.

Index

actors 5, 8, 9, 15, 31, 37, 38, 40–42, 47, 48, 57, 66, 71
Altenburg, T. 51
analytical framework
    labor agency, conceptualizing 67–71
    limitations 19–20
Atlanta Agreement 74
Azmeh, S. 22

Bair, J. 40
Bangladesh Garments Manufacturers and Exporters Association (BGMEA) 27
Barrientos, S. 55
Better Cotton Initiative (BCI) 39
Blowfield, M.E. 2
Böhm, S. 98
branded buyers 69
branded companies 7, 65, 66, 69, 80, 83, 84, 86, 88
brands 5, 12, 23–5, 27–9, 31–3, 36, 38, 64, 72, 101, 103, 104
brand supplier factories 27
brand suppliers 27
buyer-centric approaches 2, 3
buyer codes of conduct 25, 26, 29, 36
buyer perspectives 9–10, 23–39
    compliance paradigm
        drivers 24–5
        expanded compliance paradigm and limitations 29–31
        main features 25–8
        theoretical underpinnings 28–9
    cooperation paradigm
        drivers 31
        limitations 35–6
        main features 32–4
        theoretical underpinnings 34–5
buyer (ir)responsibility 2
buyers 4, 6, 7, 9, 10, 12, 13, 15–20, 23, 29, 30, 32, 41, 42, 90

interests of 6, 8–10, 13, 16–18, 88, 90, 92

Campling, L. 97
Cashore, B. 93, 94
Chan, C.K. 13
child labor 22–4, 27, 30, 39, 43, 45, 46, 55, 72, 73, 94
child workers 47, 55, 61
circular economy 88, 92, 99–101, 103
    initiatives 100, 101
circularity 99, 100, 103
cluster-based suppliers 104
cluster-centered perspectives 49–63
    clusters, chains and women's social downgrading 56–9
    industrial clusters 51–6
        cluster-based firms, proximity 53–6
        collective CSR action 59–61
    social up/downgrading, gendered nature 51–6
cluster integration 51, 52, 59
clusters 51–63, 72, 74
cluster workforce 58, 59
coalition 24, 31
codes of conduct 9, 10, 17, 18, 23, 24, 29, 30, 32, 41
collective bargaining 3, 18, 46, 63, 64, 69, 79, 105
compliance 20, 23, 25, 27, 29, 37–9, 42, 87, 88, 90, 93
compliance-based paradigm 25–9
compliance paradigm 20, 23–7, 29, 31, 37, 90
consolidated supplier perspective 21, 41, 47
constraining worker agency 71
contractors 67, 72, 73, 94
cooperation approach 10, 16–18, 65
cooperation approaches 12, 20, 35, 38

cooperation paradigm 19, 20, 23, 24,
   31–7, 88, 90
cooperative paradigm 32–4, 65, 85, 86,
   103
corporate codes of conduct 6, 27, 29, 30,
   32, 37, 40, 42, 64, 68
corporate sustainability 97
COVID-19 1–3, 6, 20, 25–9, 31, 33,
   35–7, 50, 64, 65, 85, 89–90

D'Cruz, P. 5
De Neve, G. 14, 54, 67
D'Haese, M. 85
disarticulations perspective 57
Distelhorst, G. 10
domestic value chains 29

economies 11, 12, 52, 105
elections 79, 80
employment 7, 13, 15–17, 49, 54, 63, 65,
   67, 77, 85, 86
enabling rights 63
environmental due diligence 94, 95
environmental issues 5, 48, 97
environmental upgrading 98, 99, 105
ethical trade 5
European Commission 41, 42, 95
European Union 42, 94–6, 99
export-oriented factories 25, 31

factory management 32, 33, 36, 78, 80
factory workers 34
female migrant workers 14, 53
first-tier suppliers 9, 10, 15–17, 19, 61,
   90
football stitchers 14, 72, 73, 75, 76
fringe benefits 75–7, 81
Frynas, J.G. 2

Gansemans, A. 85
garment factories 21, 26, 47
garment workers 10, 64
Gereffi, G. 7, 8, 15, 61
giant contractors 11, 22
global buyers 23, 32, 37, 42, 43, 46, 54,
   58, 61
global climate change 97–9
Global North 1, 17, 19–21, 41, 46,
   48–50, 64, 89–90, 100–102

global production networks 34, 35
Global South 1, 3, 7, 12–13, 21, 24, 41,
   44, 45, 48, 50, 51, 89–91, 95, 96,
   100, 104, 105
governments 44, 45, 48, 64, 88, 89, 91–7,
   104, 105

Hammer, N. 65, 67
Havice, E. 97
Henderson, J. 79
hidden value chains 59
Hoffman, P.S. 10
home-based women workers 59, 61, 73
horizontal relations 7, 13–15, 17–19,
   67, 77
Horner, R. 92, 94
Hughes, A. 71, 82
human rights 94–7

Indian government 96, 97
industrial clusters 21, 40, 48–53, 55, 57,
   59–63
informal labor agency 4
integrated analytical model 15
   captive governance 17–18
   hierarchical governance 18–19
   market-based relations 15–16
   relational governance 16–17
international brands 68, 72, 75, 84, 99
international buyers 9, 16, 17, 19, 34, 45,
   58, 67, 68, 84

joint action 52, 53, 55, 61, 62, 81
joint interests 7, 13, 15, 18, 20, 69

Khan, A. 45
Khara, N. 14
Knorringa, P. 50
Kramer, M.F. 43
Krishnan, A. 98

labor agency 3, 4, 18, 20, 21, 65–70, 85,
   86, 89, 91
large buyers 18, 42
large-scale suppliers 11, 20
legislation 94–7, 100
Lindgreen, A. 22, 40
local firms 52, 53, 56, 60, 61, 67
local supplier factories 67, 69, 80

Lund-Thomsen, P. 14, 22, 40, 92, 96

male factory-based workers 75
mature cluster integration 51, 58, 59
mature clusters 51, 52, 56–9
mature industrial clusters 52–4, 56–9,
      61, 62
Meyer-Stamer, J. 51
Mezzadri, A. 53, 60
migrant workers 1, 26, 85

Nadvi, K. 22, 50, 51
national labor laws 18, 24, 32, 83
national media 77, 83–4
Neilson, J. 6
NGOs 5, 8, 9, 24, 25, 34, 39, 40, 69–71,
      80–83, 100, 101, 105
Nike 39, 65–6, 72–8, 80, 82, 84–6
      football manufacturing operations
            73–7
Noman, M. 103
non-branded international buyers 72
non-compliance 23, 26, 27, 29, 30, 37, 84

OECD 94
Oka, C. 86, 105
optimum point 12, 13, 15–19

Pakistani labor law 66, 84
Palpacuer, F. 40
particular factories 33
Pasquali, G. 93, 94
PILER 81
policy implications 88, 101
      brands and retailers 101–3
      suppliers 103–4
      workers, labor unions and
            governments 104–5
Ponte, S. 95, 98
Porter, M.E. 43
Pritchard, B. 6
private partnerships 5, 71
private-sector consultants 69, 77–8, 80,
      84
public issues 44, 45
Pyke, F. 92

Rasche, A. 44
relational governance 16–18

research agendas, 2030 91–101
retailers 24, 25, 27–30, 32, 36–9, 95,
      102–4
Riisgaard, L. 65, 67
Ruwanpura, K. 68

safety risks 59, 85
Saga Sports 74, 82
Sandee, H. 52
Schmitz, H. 51
Selwyn, B. 68
shared value 41–3, 47
shop stewards 79–81, 84
Sialkot, Pakistan
      constrained agency, horizontal
            relations 77–84
      Nike's football manufacturing
            operations 73–7
Silver, B. 70
Silverstar 72–6, 78–81, 84
      factory 77, 78, 83
      management 78–81
      stitchers 73, 75, 76, 78–83
      workers 75–8, 80
SMEs 12, 16, 17, 20, 22
social dialogue 64
social downgrading 51–6, 63
social responsibilities 5, 40, 64, 89
social upgrading 51–6, 63
South Asia 60, 99–101
stakeholding 70, 71, 82, 86, 87
Sunley, P. 70, 82
supplier-centered approach 3, 21, 41
supplier-centered perspectives 40–48
      CSR in GVCS 47–8
      European Commission definitions,
            CSR 41–4
      imperialism and greenwashing, CSR
            45–6
      political CSR (PCSR) 44–5
supplier compliance 25, 30
supplier interactions 16
supplier management 24, 32
supplier perspectives 6, 11–13, 16, 42,
      43, 45–8
supplier squeezes 2, 95
supplier value chains 28
supply chains 5, 72, 94

technology 51, 62
Tendler, J. 63
textile value chains 100–102
training factory workers 66

United Kingdom Ethical Trade Initiative
    (UK-ETI) 5

value chains 27–30, 36, 39, 43, 46, 62,
    92, 98–101, 104
  governance 7, 8, 61
  struggles 6, 8, 9

Wills, J. 70, 78
women 50–63
women workers 21, 49–52, 54–62, 91
  social upgrading of 21, 51, 52, 62,
    91
work councils 78–80
worker

interests 4, 7, 10, 14, 15, 18
interviews 79, 81
perspectives 6, 7, 13–16, 66, 90
worker agency 7, 65–7, 69, 70, 79, 88
  facilitating 84, 86
worker-centered perspectives 64–87
  analytical framework 67–71
  constrained agency 77–84
  methodology 72–3
  national media 83–4
  NGOs 80–83
  Nike's football manufacturing
    operations 73–7
  private-sector consultants 77–8
  work councils 78–80
workers
  exercise labor agency 14
  labor 2, 60, 70
Workers' Rights Consortium 25
Wright, E.O. 70, 80

Printed and bound by CPI Group (UK) Ltd, Croydon, CR0 4YY

16/04/2025

14658433-0002